Thank God It's Monday!

Thank God It's Monday!

How to Love the Job You Do

Sarah Berry

HELP YOURSELF

Copyright © 2003 by Sarah Berry

First published in Great Britain in 2003

The right of Sarah Berry to be identified as the Author of
the Work has been asserted by her in accordance
with the Copyright, Designs and Patents Act 1988.

10 9 8 7 6 5 4 3 2 1

British Library Cataloguing in Publication Data
A record for this book is available from the British Library

ISBN 0 340 78734 1

Typeset by Avon Dataset Ltd, Bidford-on-Avon, Warks

Printed and bound in Great Britain by
Bookmarque Ltd., Croydon, Surrey

The paper and board used in this paperback are natural recyclable
products made from wood grown in sustainable forests.
The manufacturing processes conform to the environmental
regulations of the country of origin.

Hodder & Stoughton
A Division of Hodder Headline Ltd
338 Euston Road
London NW1 3BH
www.madaboutbooks.com

This book is dedicated to all my clients and all those career-minded individuals who are looking to achieve greater fulfilment and satisfaction from work.

Contents

CONTENTS

Acknowledgements

With love and special thanks to my close family David, Peter, Olivia and Henry, my friend Carey and all the staff at Hodder & Stoughton including Lorraine Keating, Julie Hatherall and my honest, direct and professional editor Judith Longman.

Introduction

Thank God It's Monday! is about getting the most from your job and your work. It provides you with an opportunity to unravel your career purpose, dreams and aspirations and to commit to actioning these today. The book helps you deal with any outdated or ineffective work beliefs to arrive at a point of childlike expectation and joy about your working week. The focus is on 'you', your power and your unique work contribution so that you can become *more purposeful* and loving in your approach to work.

People who 'love their job' exude energy, motivation, inspiration, contentment and success. Their vision is to make a difference in their job and they action their vision through love rather than through control, aggression, position or power. Love is power and it makes the person adopting its force appear special, super-human, extraordinary, gifted or simply just plain lucky. This is partly due to the fact that the person who chooses 'love' as their driving force has an easier time than those people who choose the other shorter-term options. Love requires less effort and force and it opens up more options for the individual. Options such as personal fulfilment, personal satisfaction and personal contribution.

Love helps the individual to understand and appreciate their own value work-wise and leads them to achieve greater and greater things. However, the cut and thrust of the business world is often 'blind' to the power of 'love' because there is often just not time for it. The focus is then on self and no one else. When the focus is self, it is all about getting the most things for yourself. Things such as the pay cheque, the bonus, the perks, the holidays and the things you can buy for yourself. There is nothing wrong with 'having it all for me' but it can leave you feeling isolated, empty, and maybe even a bit guilty. When your role is how your daily work activities can make a difference to other people's lives, then the focus is love. You can still have what you desire with this approach and you'll feel good about yourself and your actions in the process. Thus, this book will help you love and be passionate towards your job.

People who love their job and are passionate about their work and career are your greatest inspiration. They are in your life for a reason and can offer you:

- A vision of what you'd like to become
- An insight into having a job you'd really like
- A sneak preview at the evolving you
- Great inspiration
- And a reason to get started!

So, people who love their work stimulate others who find their job less rewarding to reflect about work. The self-reflection process is all about improving things but some people can get drawn into the snap game – the game of matching salaries, perks and bonuses; the comparison game – the game of weighing up the best boss, company or person; and there is also the denial game – the game of knocking anything that is different to your current situation.

Analysing and comparing your job against other people's lot, as you know only too well, isn't the long-term solution. It leads only to justifying your job position or background, raising or dashing your hopes or feeling good or bad about your current circumstances. In essence, it means that you have got caught up in the emotion surrounding your job situation. If you do find yourself being drawn down this route about having or doing something better job-wise then just accept that you want more and you want it badly. But, you see, wanting it, dreaming about it, or hoping to be successful isn't enough. It is too weak in terms of a solution. Having and doing a job that fulfils you is all about clarity. So, you have to start to become very honest about what you want job-wise. Therefore is real job fulfilment about:

- Having a 'top' job or a high profile?
- Having more money?
- Achieving a greater level of self-esteem?
- Achieving freedom?
- Being more powerful?
- Being regarded as special, important or even wonderful?
- Being recognised for your work and achievements?
- Achieving a title or a name for yourself?
- Becoming more 'satisfied' about your work?
- Creating the lifestyle you desire?
- Helping people who are less fortunate than yourself?
- Or creating more purpose to your work?

The fact is, when you feel good about your job you begin to look better and achieve a greater level of personal satisfaction. Whatever you feel would make you more fulfilled job-wise can be achieved. So, if you are seeking to improve your income you'll need to look hard at your beliefs about money. Equally if you are seeking to create more purpose to your work you'll need to establish what a job with real meaning 'means' to you. If you are looking to improve your lifestyle, you'll need to focus on and do *more* of what you really enjoy both at work and at home. This book will put you on the path to achieving your personal goals, dreams and aspirations. The key to developing 'passion' about your job is to be open, self-aware and willing to work upon yourself – ideally on a day-to-day basis.

The self-development questionnaire in Chapter 3 will give you an opportunity to take a safe, close, in-depth look at yourself, your job, your actions, your attitudes, your patterns and help you highlight what you need to focus your energy on improving.

Energy is often described as high, low or as fluctuating. The energy you have for your work is directly related to how fulfilled you are by your job. In order to achieve what you are looking for you will need to have the energy to 'do' something about your current circumstances. If your energy is high, great! And if your energy could do with a boost you'll get the chance to build your energy so that you can become more committed, upbeat, exciting, fun and giving as a person.

Your search for job fulfilment is all about 'you' and discovering any lost or forgotten part of you. It involves activity, change and most of all long-term commitment. Commitment and the mere mention of it can make people feel excited, worried, energised, uncertain, upbeat or even fearful. Commitment can also raise concerns about whether it will all work out for you and whether it is worth the risk and effort.

Commitment is about making choices and letting go of things that aren't in your best interest. Things that you may have believed to date have helped keep you together or in control but as you'll discover this is not always the case. Commitment forces you to stop and look forward at your future and to imagine how it could really 'be' for you. It is a fast, amazing and exciting process. For you can have in your mind today what you desire and once visualised it is then up to you to decide whether or not you are going to create it. All sorts of issues may crop up to stop you committing to taking the chance to do something about your circumstances. The commonest issues are time and money.

Time can be a big issue because it forces you to think about whether your quest for 'more' is a worthwhile investment. Perhaps you are already 30, 40, 50, 60 and are concerned about whether there is time for you to change and receive any benefit as a result. Time never runs out. It is an infinite source and it is only your perception of time that may cause you to feel impatient or frustrated.

Money and when the payback will be could also stop you from making any sort of commitment. Rest assured though, you'll be paid back for all your efforts as long as you 'give' first and up-front. You just have to decide what you want to receive and how much, then *give* of yourself fully and unconditionally. However, try to have no attachment to the outcome or result, for your role is to learn your lessons and to become 'more' of a worker and by allowing yourself to be flexible, your learning will be so much easier.

Commitment therefore is all about your ability to step forward to see and create the bigger and better you and make any changes in ways that are best for you too. All you have to decide is, 'Do I want to commit to this long-term?' and 'Am I prepared to do what is required of me?' Most of all, 'Am I prepared to stick at this in spite of any possible setbacks or failings?'

Becoming passionate about your work is all about making a lasting difference to you, your job and your long-term career, which will uplift, transform and benefit you far more than you perhaps ever dreamt possible. Remember it is as easy to be motivated, inspirational and exciting as it is to be dull, boring and depressing. It is your choice as to which one you become. Commit to what you can in the book and most of all enjoy the experience.

Now let's talk about you

You have decided to do something about your current job situation. Situations such as being threatened with redundancy, losing a job, being bored by work, looking for a shift in career direction or just looking for more from work can spur people on to do something positive about the circumstances they find themselves in. What-ever your current circumstances you know that this experience is about you, and what options are open to you in order for you to make the best choices and/or changes bringing about more enjoy-ment, satisfaction and job fulfilment for you.

Your job is made up of many, many different tasks, some of which generate feelings of pleasure, excitement, power, importance, worth and self-esteem and some of which generate feelings of pain, exhaustion, boredom, frustration, anger and maybe even negativity. However, what you experience is important and how you wish to turn your learnings into positive experiences is key to your job satisfaction. This book will help you to discover more about yourself and show you how you can create what you want to give to your job and receive from your job in return, in order to provide you with the necessary passion, satisfaction and fulfilment.

The mistake most people make when facing a job crisis is that they focus too heavily on the 'get' part of the equation and not on the 'give' part enough. Hence, dissatisfied workers are those that feel they don't:

- Earn enough money
- Get enough perks
- Have enough opportunities
- Receive enough praise and recognition
- Have enough holiday or time off
- Feel appreciated enough
- Or get what they want from their job.

The truth is though, if you feel that you don't 'get' enough from your job then that is important and needs to be focused upon. Equally though if the 'get' bit isn't enough, then you need to look hard at the 'give' bit. The 'give' and 'get' bits need to be equally balanced if you want to achieve personal job satisfaction. Many people stop giving to their job because they don't feel that they are receiving enough in return. Others stop giving because they feel that they have given enough already. Others stop giving because they genuinely feel that they have very little left to give.

Most people avoid getting clear about what 'giving and receiving' really means job-wise because they are perhaps uncomfortable about something. Change and the concern about what is involved or the fear about making a mistake also cause people to stop giving. Hence, getting clear about your job situation ultimately means having to face the truth. The truth that you could be so much 'more' in terms of an employee or a worker.

Yes, it is a positive truth although many people don't view it this way because they ask themselves negative questions. When 'having or being more' is viewed as a fear people ask themselves questions such as 'Why me?', 'Will it really work out?', 'Do I really deserve all that?' When 'being more' is viewed as a positive it involves facing up to what you need and want by asking yourself positive questions. Questions such as:

- What do I need to do?
- What part of me do I need to change?
- What could help me do, achieve or be that?
- What is stopping me?
- What do I need to let go of?
- When am I going to start?
- What am I going to do when I succeed?
- Whose support do I need?
- Who can help me achieve this goal, plan or target?

Then accepting the truth involves the commitment bit. The realisation and desire that you need to commit yourself to becoming more and this may involve making some changes to the way you currently perform your job. But remember it is commitment with a big 'C' and change with a little 'c'. Commitment is the only way forward because the only other option is to remain an average employee, a mediocre employee or even a dissatisfied employee!

Most people want to become 'more' in terms of an employee or worker but, and it is a big BUT, they are always waiting for someone else to tell them how good, brilliant or capable they are. The reason for this is that the person is afraid to recognise their individual value, contribution and power. Is this the case with you too? Becoming 'more' is all about moving forward and changing the pattern of the past. It is about seeing and accepting yourself as you currently are and allowing yourself to unfold, develop and mature daily within your job and role so that you are gradually becoming so much 'more' in terms of a worker. For there is no such thing as 'doing the right thing' or 'taking a certain path or route'; it has more to do with learning about yourself and giving what you have learnt about yourself to your job and receiving your just reward in return. Hence the more you work on yourself and give to your job, the more you will receive from your job in return. Then the balance of giving and receiving will be restored.

The issue of truth

'Giving and receiving' is closely linked to the issue of truth. A job crisis, a job change, a loss of a job or a time when a job doesn't fulfil you, is a period of time when you can self-reflect, assess and ultimately 'see' the truth about yourself and your circumstances. Most of the time the truth gets hidden and lost under the burden and responsibility of work itself. Perhaps because it is easier to speak your truth sometimes than at other times. Perhaps there is a concern about how other people would react if you spoke about what you really felt. Or perhaps you think that you are the only person who feels the way you do.

If you allow it, your truth can get overlooked at work in the hype of activity and then you run the risk of suffering. Suffering could mean that you:

- Overwork
- Sacrifice things that are important to you
- Promise yourself and others things and never get around to it
- Have little time for other people
- Make excuses for your behaviour
- Put up with things that you wish you didn't have to
- 'Keep in' with people rather than doing what is right for you
- Question yourself a lot of the time
- Get speaking your truth muddled up with confrontation.

When you look for an answer to a job-related issue, quite a lot may come up for you to deal with because your truth may have been lying dormant for a while. For the big temptation with the 'truth' is to see it, hear it, feel it and then to hide it because it may not be convenient to deal with it when it appears. Then you may have to hide your truth by swallowing your words or keeping quiet. If you do respond in this way then your truth is hidden deep within your body and then there is always the risk that it may creep out later as pain, anger, frustration, criticism of yourself or others, resentment, lethargy, doubt, lack of trust or even as loneliness.

Hiding the truth at work is so common. For there is a big 'illusion' that employees have to do the right thing and sometimes speaking the truth at work is deemed to be the wrong thing to do. Speaking honestly and frankly has a risk that the message will be heard and may be tricky for the other person to accept. This other person may be the boss, a colleague, a client, a customer, a friend or someone important to your future career prospects. When the truth makes others feel uncomfortable there is usually a period of silence, which could last for minutes, hours, days, or years while the truth is absorbed and reflected upon. Silence, in itself, isn't painful but it can make people feel so uncomfortable that there is then a huge temptation to 'fill that silence'. People fill the silence either unconsciously or out of habit by taking back their words, apologising, making an excuse or covering up in some way. Thus, speaking the truth is so powerful that it can lead people to justify the situation in either a calm or frantic way. Then, the message or truth, can get lost and people get caught up in all the emotion around the truth itself. People then harbour feelings about the situation that may be left unresolved and hence left to fester and possibly build. *This is where the pain is, in the unresolved bits, not in the truth itself.* Then the truth arouses issues of security.

When the truth is unresolved then either party can begin to feel threatened by the truth. A period of 'cooling-off' usually takes place when neither party really knows what to do but both parties usually experience similar things. This period is a time of self-reflection or perhaps even self-doubt. It is therefore probable that both parties will be feeling things like:

- What does he/she feel about me?
- What or how does this affect our working relationship?
- What should I be doing here?
- Is this my fault?
- How could I have prevented this?
- How could I have handled this better?
- Will he/she treat me differently?
- And perhaps even, do I need this relationship any more?

When you or someone else gets caught up in the 'emotion' about the truth then *STOP*. Stopping helps you to recognise and to begin to accept what is happening. It helps you avoid the temptation to respond to the emotion and to get stuck there by holding on to perhaps your feelings of anger, frustration, sadness or whatever it is for you. *You see, the focus of your attention needs to be on your truth and what you need to learn, not the emotion around it.* The key thing to be aware of is how you experience the truth. Do you experience your truth by speaking about it, as in the above example? Do you have people who share their experiences with you? Do you experience your truth by coming face to face with it in written messages, either in books, signs, billboards, newspapers or magazines? Or do you come across your truth by having someone tell you the truth face to face?

You will experience it in a way that is powerful and enlightening to you and in a way that is designed to bring out the 'best' in you. The thing with the truth is, try to 'hear', 'see' and 'understand' the message and work out what you need to do as a result, rather than getting caught up in all the emotion around the truth. Tricky, I know; however, it is possible and it is better for you in the long run.

There are a lot of emotions surrounding any form of truth and it is this emotion that can arouse your feelings of security. It is this potential threat to security that stops many people from speaking up or acting upon their truth at work, because perhaps they fear:

- Losing that pay increase, promotion or opportunity
- Being dropped from certain functions, meetings or groups
- Being treated differently as a result.

Yes, your truth can change things, but have you forgotten that those changes are to help you to become 'more' of a person? Next, it is important to gain an appreciation of what you *do* when you feel that being honest would threaten your 'security' in any way. For work and the process of work has the potential to make you feel needed, wanted and secure. Security for most people is to do with their bank balance. The balance that at the end of the month makes them feel important, powerful, successful and that their pain and efforts were all worthwhile. For money and the flow of money can quash any feelings of vulnerability. For example, a bad week at work or a bad month can be put aside when the pay cheque arrives.

Being and feeling vulnerable is vital to achieving job fulfilment. Vulnerability is your inner code and if listened to and responded to, it can bring out the best in you. However, most people feel it all right, but they avoid looking at it in any depth. So they may choose to walk away from situations, to avoid truthful discussions, to avoid people who make them feel their own vulnerability, to work harder to prove themselves or to focus on getting more for themselves. In fact they probably even think that everything is OK but they are holding a lot within.

Your vulnerability is there for one reason, which is to help you focus on giving more. It is there to stop you withdrawing, hiding and running away and to help you answer the 'call' to give more of yourself to your job and others.

Hence, if your vulnerability and truth get buried in any way, the biggest thing that gets lost is 'you' and your potential for job fulfilment. If this happens, you may perhaps begin to focus on a different sort of truth – a fix-it sort of truth or a have-it sort of truth – in the hope that your feelings of vulnerability will go away. And they may disappear for a while until they get jabbed again at a later date. As the jabbing gets stronger, it will be harder for you to ignore these feelings. This book will help you to do something positive about your feelings of vulnerability and to take positive daily action.

Love has to exist if you want to achieve any sort of job fulfilment and success. You have therefore to really love what you do, offer and contribute to the work world. Loving, in relation to work or jobs, is all about doing something that is special and meaningful to you. It is about being able to feel good about your ability to give and offer your uniqueness to the work world. It is about taking the risk to be yourself and to risk 'loving' others within your day-to-day activities. It is about being open, receptive and responsive to the needs and desires of others. It is about being able to give and receive, thereby making your individual mark on the work world. Yes, it is about 'you' but not to the exclusion or detriment of others. Most of all it is about taking the risk to 'share' your true self with others and to feel and to act upon your vulnerability in the process. Therefore this book is all about recognising your truth and acting upon it. So there may be some habits for you to break and some self-made blocks to take down. It is vitally important, however, that you remain in tune with your thoughts, feelings and emotions at all times, so that you can be true to yourself and respond accordingly. It is about seeing and developing yourself so that you are able to place your security firmly in your hands – in your talents, skills and uniqueness – so that you can become 'more' in terms of an employee or worker on a day-to-day basis.

Remember your attention in future needs to be on yourself and how you can give more of yourself to your job. If this is the case then you will begin to realise that you do create your work experiences in order to learn what you need to develop 'more of' in terms of your skills, traits or personal qualities. And as you work on yourself and with others you will discover that 'becoming more' is a continual process of giving and receiving.

Giving of yourself, your talents and capabilities and thereby receiving your just rewards back in return. And when you really start to enjoy your work, then recognise your achievements and allow yourself to be content, relaxed and happy and you will continue to be rewarded. As soon as you try to 'hold on' to your feelings of fulfilment or even 'question' them, they will gradually start to slip away from you. So if this happens to you, get your sense of job fulfilment back by working on yourself. Then, you'll constantly be in tune with your feelings about your job fulfilment and hence be in a position to take the necessary and effective action.

Let's begin that process of self-development, so that Monday can really become the day you cherish the most. For it is the beginning of a new week and you have the opportunity to make an impact on your and other people's working lives.

Step One – The Pain Cycle

The 'pain cycle' is the cycle that you can fall into if your job isn't all that you feel it could or ought to be. Pain refers to the feelings of frustration, irritation or lack surrounding you. Do you feel hurt by your circumstances? By recognising and acknowledging your pain and your response to it, you can then choose more empowering ways of dealing with it in the future. The type of pain that you personally experience has more to do with what you need to become 'more of' and what you may need over time to develop, rather than what you are not. If you focus on what you are not, you will feel the pain more intensely. For example, if you feel helpless in a situation you may need to identify and develop skills that you feel would help you; if you feel inadequate you may need to develop more self-confidence and self-belief; if you don't know what to say maybe you need to begin to value and trust your views and opinions more.

Your pain is what you decide is 'wrong with you, wrong about the situation or wrong about the job'. You are never stuck and you can always become more of what you already are. The choice about whether that happens is yours. The pain cycle stops or drops when you can see what you are or have been doing and how you, and you alone, are creating this cycle of pain for yourself to learn from. *Pain is a really, really positive internal sign when you begin to use it to your advantage, as it is there to give you insight into the evolving you or the evolving situation.* Use it wisely and you'll develop as a person but quash or stamp on it and you'll be rejecting a part of you and your potential forever.

Therefore feeling good about your job is all about creating a balance between pain and pleasure. Work is neither one thing nor the other but an experience of both pain and pleasure at different stages and times in your job. Hence the reason why you do need to experience both pain and pleasure in order to raise and achieve your level of job satisfaction and become 'more' in terms of an employee or worker.

Your painful experiences provide you with your greatest lessons and your pleasure experiences hold your greatest dreams, hopes, goals, feelings of joy, value and self-worth. Creating balance in your job is what you are ultimately after because it would be wrong or naïve to suggest that you can have one without the other. For example, to have only pleasure and no pain or only pain and no pleasure. If you are drawn towards 'pain' it is important to feel the pain and to experience the pain. Once you have done this, you can then gain an insight about the situation and decide what action you are going to take in order to create positive change. For example, if you feel jealous try to establish what the jealousy is all about and how you can begin to become 'more' of the thing/s that make you jealous. The diagram opposite indicates the typical cycle of pain. Can you identify with this cycle? Have you been in this cycle or are you perhaps there at the moment? Perhaps you don't identify with the words but just have an overwhelming feeling that your job or work is an uphill struggle.

Work can be a struggle and you can get caught in the cycle unless you use your painful experiences positively. However, before any positive action can be taken, it is important to understand what triggers and drives the pain in the first place and how you may be relieving the pain of your job at the moment. Only when you can see the pattern, can you choose how you can break the

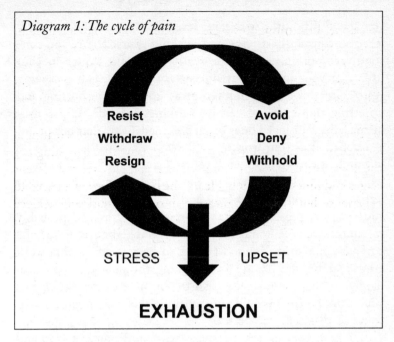

Diagram 1: The cycle of pain

cycle once and for all and step forward and become 'more' of a worker.

The workplace and the pain trigger

The workplace has changed over recent years and this has had a huge impact on you, has it not? You work longer and harder than employees did 50 years ago. More is being demanded of you today in terms of commitment, time, output, effort, travel hours and not forgetting any preparation you do at home. Do you feel that you are giving more of yourself, your personality and also your leisure time to your company or organisation?

But if this is not what you want long-term, why are you still doing it five days a week, 48 weeks a year? Are you working yourself silly? Are you finishing work so late that you spend little time with your loved ones, family and friends? Are you constantly striving and pushing yourself? Are you constantly compromising on the really important things in your life? Are you missing out on certain things, such as seeing your children or grandchildren grow up? Are you hurting and upsetting those around you by working so hard? As a consequence, do your loved ones often feel inadequate, left out or not as important as your work?

Surely it isn't right to work yourself so hard? Is it fair to those who aren't working as hard as you to feel guilty, inadequate or left out? Do you work so long and hard because it is easier for your relationships to suffer, your temper to fray and probably to some extent your health to deteriorate, than it is for the company's or organisation's targets to be missed? Is this work ethic making you happy? Is it making the people around you happy? Is this the way you wish to continue to live the rest of your working life? Would you continue this way if you knew it could be different and better?

Before answering the questions why don't you just stop and make a commitment about when you are going to take that well-earned break? You need it after all, don't you? Have you been promising it to yourself now for the past year or maybe it is two years now or maybe even five years? However long it is, it is almost guaranteed that it is likely to be an extremely long time – far longer than you would care to remember or be reminded of!

Isn't it time you stopped and reassessed your work life for a while? Isn't it time you did things differently? Time to stop getting up early, rushing to work, rushing at work all day, and working right up until the time when you crash into bed literally exhausted by your work and experiences of your day. Then you sleep a few hours and begin the whole process in earnest all over again and your life has literally been replaced by your addiction to your *job*.

But why? What has happened to you, because after all, this isn't the way you wanted it to be back then, is it? What is your obsession or your need to work so long and hard? Have you gone crazy? Are you perhaps so materialistic now that you just have to have that next luxury item? Or is your work situation more to do with circumstances?

Sure, there are many factors at play here. Yes, most people enjoy luxury and having a good time but there is more to do with the work obsession than this. Much of the work ethic has to do with the significant changes that have taken place in technology over recent years. Changes that you have been a part of and benefited from but, none the less, these changes have significantly impacted your life and lifestyle. Let's look now at these technological changes and appreciate how these huge changes have affected you.

Twenty years ago a leading professor at the University of Sheffield predicted that by the turn of the century people would have little need to actually communicate and talk to one another face to face. They would use machines instead. At the time, many people regarded his views as ridiculous, bizarre and a little far-fetched. But today in this highly instant and technological world his views may not receive the same amount of criticism or cynicism as they did then, for now it is a fact. Computers, machines and advances in technology have made life at work much more efficient, effective and faster but the impact has been on you and your life.

So although in theory 'fulfilment' could be a natural part of your work in reality this isn't the case, because have you forgotten what it really feels like? Do you feel energised and content about your working life? Have you got caught up in this instant, efficient and fast business world? Does this mean that you have become disconnected from your sense of you? Deep within you there still exists a place where there is purpose, contentment and a sense of peace and calm. You just need to rediscover it again. Rediscovering pleasure is all about rediscovering the lost part of you, the part of you that has got lost in all your frenzy of activity.

Since the Second World War, the business world has been expanding at a faster and faster pace. A pace that is difficult for you to keep up with long-term. The systems in place and computers help you to achieve more and more within a day but they also produce a sense of expectancy about achievement. Is this the case for you? Do you run your life according to a 'To-Do List?' As the famous philosopher once said, 'Modern man is literally mesmerised by his own activity.' Are you being pulled along almost automatically by the activity in the business world? Activity that leaves you striving for more stimulating experiences and activities?

All this activity, in time, can lead you to feel that unless you have this constant amount of daily stimulation then your job is boring, dull or unimportant. So your mind begins to demand this stimulation and in order to cope and keep up, you force yourself to go faster, work even harder and cram even more in. For a while activity will give you a 'buzz'. It has a positive effect but after a while there is a huge risk of imbalance. This imbalance is as a result of the outer forces demanding that you do more and be more. Your inner forces, at the same time, will remind you that this activity is making you feel perhaps tired, exhausted, empty, old or even disillusioned. In the beginning the activity filled you up and made you feel good but over time it can begin to create internal conflict and a state of imbalance.

At work today, there are more and more things for you to control, manage and hold up. Do you even feel out of control sometimes, for instance, are your finances not in balance? Are your emotions 'on hold'? Are your relationships suffering? The truth is that if this is the case, you have simply been 'pulled away' from or lost sight of some of the things that may be really important to you. Issues that will be looked at throughout the book in order to help you rediscover that sense of 'fulfilment' and 'self' once again.

The impact of your work on your attitude

The fast, slick and efficient work world allows you to do more, be more and complete more than you may have thought possible and this in itself is addictive and exciting. But as you may already be aware there is always a price to pay for these gains and that price is *seriousness*, your seriousness.

If you don't believe it, go and take another look at yourself. Look around you and notice your colleagues and associates. How often are they laughing, making a joke or seeing the funny side of things? More importantly, when did you last have a really good laugh at work? Work has become, has it not, a place of serious activity and serious business? It is a place where it is fundamentally important to get things right, do things in the right way and in the right order. It is unquestionably an environment where money is made and money is lost and it can become a life-and-death situation. There is no time or respect for those who are seen to be going at a slower pace, laughing, smiling or generally having a good time. In fact their more serious colleagues often see those who enjoy themselves as being a bit 'soft', childish or even unambitious. Have you ever criticised someone who was more light-hearted than you? For at work there is a huge emphasis on doing things according to the rules and within the specified timescales. For some, work can be a place of endurance rather than enjoyment and it is this very endurance that shows itself in the form of 'seriousness'. Seriousness then shows itself in behaviour, attitude and most of all in the lack of excitement about work.

Do you feel serious? Do you feel constrained, stressed and lacking in fulfilment? Seriousness means that you become less sensitive and caring towards yourself and others. Being fulfilled is therefore all about seeing, recognising and shedding your serious attitude (Step Two) and putting fun, acceptance and happiness back into your job. Before doing that, let's look at how you may be currently reacting and responding to being in the pain cycle. Then and only then, will you be aware of what behaviours you may need to change.

The first point of power –
recognising the pain

The first point of power is to recognise the pain. At this stage it isn't necessary to know what the pain is all about, although you may already know that. It is just about admitting to yourself that your job situation isn't quite how you want it to be at the moment. In one-to-one career sessions, clients tend to acknowledge or describe this period of self-acknowledgment in three ways, namely:

• Being at a career crossroads
• Rationalising their feelings
• Or by asking some tough questions.

Each one of these reactions will now be looked at in turn.

Being at a career crossroads

Here clients describe the need to change or the feelings of dissatisfaction as being at a career crossroads where someone has taken down all the signs. The route ahead is described as looking for another job in line with what they are currently doing with perhaps a few changes here and there, and the left and right turnings are described as their other 'new' unexplored options.

The lack of signs, or feelings of uncertainty, stop them from doing anything. Most clients in this situation have an overwhelming sense of waiting for, looking for or receiving a thunderbolt, which will point them in the right direction. While waiting for their sign they may also have a feeling that they are wasting their time and that time is running out. Most clients experience frustration and a feeling that they should and would like to be able to work all this out for themselves. The looking, waiting and talking to friends, colleagues, associates and people in positions of knowledge or power also somehow leave them feeling even more drained, confused or powerless.

Almost all of my clients ask me, 'Is it really up to me to decide which way to go? Couldn't you just tell me what to do, please?'

Rationalising feelings

Here clients describe how they feel about their job situation and how these feelings aren't going away. In fact these uncomfortable feelings are there day after day. Some clients describe it as a portion of their working life being over and that their job no longer gives them what they want any more. Other clients say that their job no longer holds the same attraction for them as it did in the past so they are no longer excited about the week ahead, awake before the alarm goes off or satisfied by the length of the weekend. Some clients find it tricky to pinpoint or to describe what is going on but that they just feel that things ought to be better than they are at present. Other clients talk about what career or job route they feel they should have pursued or followed. Some clients even describe it as a period in which they feel that time is passing them by, job pleasures seem to be few and far between and the rewards are getting smaller and smaller.

Feelings are a natural built-in alarm system and information system. Feelings, if listened to and acted upon, help a person to experience a situation fully. However, if feelings have been pushed down or not listened to for a long time, when they do stir, emerge or surface they have the ability to make an individual feel out of control and therefore slightly frightened or alarmed by their natural response system. So this is when the individual might start to rationalise their feelings. Some of the things my clients have said are:

- This is just a phase and things will get better soon.
- It is because work has been particularly tough recently. A holiday or some time off is what I need.
- It is due to the weather, the season – yes, winter is nearly over.
- This is just down to my age. I'm just going through a mini mid-life crisis.

- I'm just very restless at present. Perhaps I need to be more patient.
- Things will work out, won't they?

Tough questioning

For other clients the acknowledgment of their pain arouses many questions, memories or thoughts. These clients ask lots of revealing questions during their consultancy sessions. Questions like:

- Is this whole desire for something better down to my age?
- Is this job fulfilment thing just a phase?
- Do you think there is something wrong with me?
- Is being fulfilled about being lucky or being in the right place at the right time?
- Do you think that I am weak?
- Is having a fulfilling job about being handsome or attractive?
- Is spark provided by certain professions, such as public relations, marketing, dramatic arts, selling or the media rather than engineering, retailing, law or insurance?

Questions such as the above are positive signs that the individual is considering the options and opening up the way for change, but the questions are all focused on the negative rather than the positive.

Recognising your pain

These three ways demonstrate how most people tend to acknowledge their 'pain'. Which of these three ways do you use? Your pain is internal, mental and unique to you. It stands between you and greater things and whether it is a large or a small amount of pain, you need to acknowledge that it exists. The pain, though, is not there to embarrass, shame or humiliate you. It is there to help you to recognise that a key quality or trait is lacking or needs to be developed in order to take you to a deeper level of self-development and realisation. (Many people may resist doing their inner development work and if they do or if they give up too early, they could feel as if they have failed or as if their career development has stopped. And in effect it has, not because their career has stopped progressing but because they have chosen to stop progressing.) Is this what you want for yourself? Or are you prepared to go through the pain in order to make a huge difference to your work life? All you have to do is commit yourself to change and to doing the exercises.

Try to accept that your pain is there to guide, direct and point you in the direction of bigger and better things, which you can only realise, achieve and obtain if you and you alone do your inner work. Yes, sure, from time to time you'll feel like you must ask someone else what to do because you perceive it to be quicker. But ask yourself, 'Do they really know what I want?' And even if they do tell me, 'Will I believe it?' The truth is, by discovering about the thunderbolt yourself, you'll be convinced that 'This is my answer' and then you'll be willing to take the necessary action. For this whole process is about self-approval and self-acceptance, and you are the only person who can ever do that for yourself.

Likewise your pain may make you feel uncomfortable and you may even ask yourself why you ever started looking inwards. For at times it may feel as if it is the 'wrong' thing to be doing or as if you are not getting anywhere. The truth is, though, your journey from pain towards pleasure is all about you and your job. It may be a slow, a quick, a bumpy or a smooth ride but above all it'll be a ride far better than you ever expected. It is going to be a journey of truth and self-reflection, and one that is really worth making. Rest assured, you will be able to deal with your journey and that it has presented itself at the 'perfect' time for you, your personal development and future. You'll arrive at the place where you feel truly happy, comfortable and at peace. The place where you can be true to yourself and the place where you truly deserve to be.

The second point of power – clarifying your feelings

The second point of power is to describe and clarify your feelings. Being in a job that doesn't inspire you, as indicated earlier, is very common and happens to everyone within their working life but what is important is how it makes you feel. Around the ages of 28, 35 and 45 you may experience 'a need' to do some self-development work. If this development work isn't done or is ignored, then frustration, suffering and of course job vegetation can set in. When you start your inner work will depend upon how much you enjoy it.

Your pain or lack of enthusiasm about your work is always centred on your perception of 'lack'. A lack of something that you feel you need in and from your job. The self-development questionnaire in Chapter 3 clearly highlights all the areas that you will need to focus your attention on. It will give you a global and completely unbiased view about the extent and depth of your necessary inner work. For now though, before you complete the questionnaire, what is your perception about your pain? Circle or tick the issues that are relevant to you. Is your 'pain' or lack of passion about your work centred around:

- Money
- Prestige
- Respect
- Value and self-worth
- Progression and opportunity
- Power
- Calmness
- Clarity
- Quality
- Safety
- Professionalism
- Recognition
- Relationships

- Balance of work and home life
- Or something else?

Now that you have identified your issues, it is important that you acknowledge how you feel. How do you feel about no longer knowing why you are feeling the way you are feeling? Do you feel, 'Is this it?' about your work? Is this what you've got to endure for the remaining five, ten, 15 or 20 years?

Did these feelings creep into your life suddenly or over a period of time? These feelings, if acknowledged, can be managed and put to good use. On the other hand, feelings that are left, suppressed or ignored will keep coming back until they are acknowledged.

The words below are there to help you highlight exactly what it is you feel about your job situation. Circle or tick the words you feel describe your feelings the best.

Feelings about work

• Lost	• Dissatisfied	• Confused
• Frustrated	• Anxious	• Beaten
• Desperate	• Unhappy	• Bored
• Fed-up	• Cross	• Disillusioned
• Cheated	• Stuck	• Trapped
• Doing time	• Wasting time	• In the wrong place

How did you get on? Were you able to identify how you feel about what you are experiencing at present? This is the phase that many of my clients have described as the 'Is this it?' phase.

If the above words were too strong or not relevant to you, try to describe your feelings by completing the following sentences. In my job:

- I have a sense of

- I feel

- I am aware of

- I experience

Understanding your feelings will help you to become more in touch with yourself and help you to create and take advantage of your job opportunities. You need your feelings to help you deal with the work world. For it is your feelings that tell you when someone is lying to you, taking advantage of you or when something just isn't quite right. When harnessed, your feelings can put you on track to achieving exactly what you want.

The third point of power – reactions to pain

The third point of power is to notice your reactions to your 'pain' and whether these reactions are positive or negative ones. What actions are you taking as a result? Let's look now at all the possible negative reactions that you may have or be experiencing. There are many responses to dealing with the 'pain' or the feeling of loss, inadequacy or defeat, but the issue is how to deal with it positively; otherwise you can remain stuck in the phase or absorbed by your pain.

Denial

Denial is one of the most common reactions to feeling any pain about a job or a career issue. The denial phase involves withdrawing, being engrossed in something else, blocking out the pain by closing down, changing the subject or refusing to talk about the issue. Here the person may try to put off the inevitable situation of assessing their job situation. Therefore the person would perhaps book a holiday, try to socialise more, go out for Sunday lunch, eat more healthily, or try to get fit. However, whatever diversions the person tries to use, those niggling and uncomfortable thoughts about the job come back. In the denial phase the person would have thoughts along the lines of the following:

- I'll deal with this later.
- I don't need to be fulfilled at work at the moment.
- My job is not that bad.
- I didn't think this would happen to me.
- I am doing OK just as I am.
- I am not being affected by all this.

The denial reaction can be a safe, comfortable and understandable reaction if the person isn't looking for inspiration, drive and enthusiasm from the job. Some people deliberately choose to expect less from their job if 'spark' or 'excitement' is provided by another part of their life. For example, if the person is newly married, newly parenting or working on outside interests or hobbies – things that are on a higher priority list than their job or career. Under these circumstances the denial phase offers individuals an opportunity to take a break or a breather in their career by plateauing for a period of time while their focus is on other things. But the plateau periods cause problems when the person hasn't actually chosen to plateau. Then the denial reaction is almost a self-protection mechanism because the phase isn't being fully understood or appreciated.

When the plateau period or a job loss is inflicted upon the person rather than the person choosing it, then it can be a deeply painful time unless the person allows their feelings to come up and recognises, acknowledges and acts upon them.

If your response to your job issue is denial ask yourself, 'What am I protecting?' Give yourself time to absorb what is happening to you and honour your feelings. Look for as much factual information or help as you can and be patient with yourself. Your response will and can change if you allow yourself to 'feel' your feelings.

Anger

Anger or feeling angry about a job situation is another common reaction. Anger, just like any other emotion, is OK and can be dealt with positively, although there is often a great cultural myth that it is wrong to be angry or to feel angry. Is this true for you? The real issue with anger, however, is how it is handled and managed. Anger, just like every other emotion, has to be dealt with; it won't just go away simply by ignoring, avoiding or apologising for it. If you are angry about your circumstances, it is necessary to understand your anger and to explore the source of your anger, which isn't as difficult as you might think. It is important to appreciate that the masculine way to deal with anger is to take action and the feminine way to deal with it is to feel it emotionally. It is the combination of both responses that brings about the best results.

The anger reaction is all about the person realising that they are angry with themself, others or authorities, and creating situations to vent their feelings. Who are you usually cross with? Is it yourself, your boss, your colleagues, your partner, parents or children or your equipment? How do you express your anger? Do you vent your feelings and frustrations? Do you just feel angry and swallow your words? Does your anger creep out as snide remarks or comments? Do you just feel resentful?

Your anger is there for a reason and again it is there to help you develop as a person. Dealing with anger is all about looking deep below the surface to the place where your needs lie. Is your need for help, love, reassurance, guidance, support or approval? Are you afraid to see it? Are you afraid to ask for help? Do you perhaps feel embarrassed that you feel the way you do? By focusing on your needs and not your anger you are helping yourself. You are above all recognising your needs and wants and then you can find more positive ways to deal with your angry feelings. Unless you acknowledge it and do something about it, your anger will grow into bitterness, resentment or more angry feelings.

Your anger is an important part of you because it allows you to understand, explore and experience a part of yourself fully. Success is achieved when you can manage your feelings and the situation, and take positive action as a result.

Dealing with anger

Talking about anger isn't enough. You need to know how to identify the triggers, clarify the feelings, and own the anger and therefore your own positive action.

- **Identifying the triggers** Everyone has and experiences triggers to their anger. For some people it is about feeling hot and bothered, squashed, agitated, quiet or not being able to listen. The trigger is a sign that you feel something and at this stage it may not be anger. Notice the feeling and acknowledge it.
- **Clarify the feeling** The next stage is to clarify how you feel. Ask yourself, 'What do I feel?' 'What is all this about?' You may need to ask yourself, 'What do I need?' Initially you may experience a buzzy, crabby or just a full feeling. Once you get used to looking at your anger you'll then be able to put words to the feelings.
- **Own the anger** This stage is vital to your personal growth because it is about you, what you feel and what you need to work upon. The simplest way to own your anger is by expressing it in terms of 'I feel'. For example, 'I feel surprised by what you said', 'I feel left out and would therefore like to discuss it', 'I

feel hurt by what happened and would therefore like to discuss it', 'I feel shocked by what I have just heard and therefore would like you to clarify it', 'I feel disappointed that my recommendations were not considered and therefore would like the opportunity to discuss them with you.'

By owning your anger and by expressing it through 'I feel' instead of 'You made me feel', your message will be heard and the person is unlikely to feel at fault, under attack or threatened. By taking responsibility for your angry feelings and actions you show that you are prepared to keep the lines of communication open and are looking for ways to resolve the situation in the best possible way for all concerned. Your anger can therefore be channelled in a constructive way rather than directed at someone or something. For by showing your anger towards others who you perceive as being luckier, richer, more capable, more well-liked, more educated or talented than yourself, you are simply giving your power and energy away and you'll remain feeling angry and perhaps even helpless.

Once owned, your anger can then be used as a way to help you realise that you need to develop a part of yourself. The energy provided by the anger may be what you need in terms of courage or power to take that action. The self-development questionnaire will help you deal with identifying new areas for development but it may be worthwhile writing down what you feel you need to develop. For example, 'I need to develop more compassion, confidence, self-belief, detachment or conviction.' Refer to the list below and write down five things that you need to work on.

Needs inventory list

- Love
- Balance
- Clarity
- Support
- Help
- Integrity
- Advice
- Knowledge
- Power

- Adventure
- Freedom
- Perks
- Focus
- Value
- Commitment
- Fringe benefits
- Power
- Confidence
- Self-belief
- Empathy
- Equality
- Joy
- Ability to apologise
- Glamour
- Persistence
- Holiday
- Emotional maturity
- Identification with company
- Money
- Detachment
- Relationships
- Respect
- Wisdom
- Harmony
- Honesty
- Enthusiasm
- Spontaneity
- Energy
- Recognition
- Rapport
- Communication
- Compassion
- Quality
- Self-acceptance
- Relaxation

Five things I need to work on to overcome my anger:

- I need to develop or have more

- I need to develop or have more

- I need to develop or have more

- I need to develop or have more

- I need to develop or have more

Comparison

The comparison game is another common reaction to a job-related issue. The person uses this route to see if it holds any answers. Here the person might compare their lot in terms of job, opportunities, package, benefits and pension against what their friends, colleagues or acquaintances are receiving. For example, 'I have more than John/Jane or the same as Nick/Nicola so I am OK; in fact I am doing rather well.'

For a while the comparison route appears to work, especially if the person feels better than or the same as the other person, and then the feelings of irritation or frustration about the job may subside as a result. However, the thing about comparisons is that it is an addictive process and as soon as the person starts the checking routine, it has to continue; otherwise the dissatisfaction about the job comes back again. The comparison route doesn't work at all if the friend is doing better.

Do you use this route? What are you looking for? Are you willing to let go of this habit? Would you like to be 'more' in terms of a person?

Looking back in history

This reaction involves looking outside and backwards to search out an answer. On some level it involves the person entering a type of comfort state about their current circumstances because history and the circumstances of the past can't answer back and speak the truth. Here the person would be looking to confirm that their circumstances aren't that bad because others had it worse in the past, so to speak. This process helps the individual to convince themself that no action needs to be taken. Hence, why the big drama? 'I have a job, albeit a boring one', or 'It could be worse – I have a roof over my head, the kids are OK and my partner is doing all right too.' Or it could be along the lines of, 'My parents' or grandparents' working lives were tougher than mine so, hey, I'd better stop complaining.'

The thing is though, just like other reactions, this one only offers temporary relief. The feelings don't go away just because they are being pushed down or aside.

The real questions are, 'Do you want it to be and feel better?' 'Do you want to continue to use historical circumstances as your excuse?'

Covering-up

The cover-up reaction is the process that an individual will go to, in order to create the illusion that everything is OK, all right and perfect again; well, for the time being at least!

The cover-up process is about resistance; namely, 'resistance to looking at yourself'. Do you fall into the trap of cover-up? If you do then you may be doing some or all of the following:

- Not listening
- Not learning
- Not developing in the role
- Not asking questions or showing an interest
- Not being flexible
- Not communicating with others
- Not being caring or sensitive to the needs of others
- And finally not performing in the job.

Are you doing any of the above? Covering-up is easy to do and it lures the person into the illusion that it is not 'safe' to self-analyse. This may be because the person feels scared, threatened or ill-prepared in some way. So the person will avoid looking at themselves by perhaps doing some or many of the following:

- Making silly remarks or jokes
- Making excuses for their attitude, personality, behaviour or circumstances
- Running away from situations, discussions or people
- Avoiding looking at themselves through other people's eyes

- Creating disasters or situations that prevent the 'look-within' process
- Criticising others
- Denying things
- Attacking others and their character
- Telling lies or living a lie
- Pretending everything is OK
- Saying that there isn't time
- Looking to others to take responsibility for their issues.

The individual who enters the cover-up game feels the pain about their job situation but consciously chooses not to deal with it. The consequence is that people around the individual may find *them* a 'pain' because of their cover-up antics.

The cover-up process is a tempting, attractive and luring process because it appears on the surface to work. For initially no one does notice or spot the fact that the individual is making excuses, avoiding things or withdrawing from activities. Thus, it is a dangerous cycle to get involved in, for every time the individual engages in the cover-up cycle it becomes easier and easier to do and convince themself that 'no one has noticed'. Then the individual is tempted every now and then to add a few extra layers of pretence. This is to keep up the pretence and convince themself that all is under cover once again. Hence, at the moment of exposure, the individual can experience a whole range of strong emotions, namely:

- Anger
- Pain
- Sadness
- Shame
- Embarrassment
- Guilt
- Or even relief!

Some clients have even described it as strongly as 'living a lie', both at home and at work. Relief is the point of power because it offers the individual the opportunity to step forward and to self-reflect. It represents the 'letting go' process of cover-ups in which the individual has been trapped for so long.

Is there anything that you are covering up? What are you afraid of? Do cover-ups make you feel less vulnerable? There may be an uncomfortable period while you are in transition from your old ways and before you have developed your new qualities. However, remember that your vulnerability is there for a reason – to allow you to feel and experience your so-called weaknesses in order to make positive changes. Your vulnerability has the potential to make you stronger as a person – not weaker – as long as you can recognise it and do something positive about it.

The fourth point of power – how you are currently relieving your pain

The fourth point of power is to recognise how you are currently relieving your pain. What actions are you taking, and are these positive or negative ones? Do you believe your actions are positive and perhaps fail to understand why nothing changes or improves for the better?

Work, for most people, is a means to an end and therefore any job can become something that you get used to, bored by or regard in time as dull. Work and the process of work are habits. A habit is usually something, unless you are lucky, that you need to do every day. It is easy to get used to the routine and the people and thereby used to dulling your senses, expectations and aspirations. Is this true for you? Do you no longer notice your worth and contribution? Do you appreciate your employer? Do you value your work colleagues and associates? Have you become dull, heavy and negative? Do you bring enthusiasm to your job, or are you trying to force your job or your company to give it to you?

Work can be viewed as a 'struggle' of highs and lows or as a trap. Do you want to release yourself from the struggle, the chains or trap? Let's look now at how you may be choosing to relieve the burden of work at the moment. These pain relievers offer only temporary relief because they don't deal with the root cause of your pain. (These areas will be highlighted further in the self-development questionnaire.)

Pain relief or coping with pain

Listed below are three of the most common pain relievers used by people who are stuck in a career rut.

Find a new job
The first and most common way to escape from the burden of work is to look for another less painful job. A new job would offer the individual that much needed buzz or job boost. So the job search begins in earnest.

The attraction of a 'new job', whether it turns out to be an internal or an external move, has a huge pull of excitement. It offers the potential to transform the individual's working life into something much better. It offers the 'I love my job' phase – the phase when the individual feels 'alive, fresh and powerful' and is ready to give to their job and in return the individual feels valued, of worth and needed again. With new people to work with and new things to occupy the mind, it provides the desired energy, excitement and transformation the individual is seeking.

But then of course what happens is that the job becomes the norm just like the last job and after about 12 to 18 months the spark, enthusiasm and excitement fade. The newness wears off and the individual slips back into their old ways and once again the job can be regarded as not providing that necessary fulfilment.

Then as the individual initially wants and then yearns for 'that lost spark', the issue becomes one of control as they get everything back into order – into the places they believe things were before the spark went missing!

If order takes over then the individual has lost sight of the purpose of the job and therefore begins to head for the next phase, which is: 'I am beginning to hate this job.' The individual then starts to lose their sense of fun, flexibility and spontaneity and begins to wilt in their job in their attempt to be organised. Wilting employees lose their drive, stimulation and energy and gradually in time they also lose their personal ambitions, power and influence within the work environment. Soon the individual thinks that the only way that they can get out of the rut is to place even more emphasis on order, rules and safety and so they head even further towards 'hating the job'.

Once here the individual's temptation is to give up because feelings of helplessness or powerlessness can be overwhelming. The job no longer holds any meaning, spark or thrill for the person. There is though a positive and constructive side to the 'I hate my job' phase, which is the opportunity to look, question and look again at:

• How things really are
• How you have turned out
• How you would like to change.

The 'I hate my job' phase offers the opportunity to take the time to rekindle desire and to reshape things. It is the time to work things through and to use the knowledge gained to your advantage.

Are you aware that you will always look to change your job unless you get to and develop the inner and more powerful issues? Has this been your pattern to date? Have you with each successive job change become more disillusioned, frustrated or even hardened by your experiences? Have you therefore become more reliant on proof – in the form of something that you can actually see, feel or experience? Perhaps you may look for or feel you need concrete evidence before making a job change now. Do you ask yourself or others, 'Will this job work out?'

Proof, of course, is great but if you rely on proof rather than your gut instinct, there is always a risk that you could become too reliant on something other than yourself before you dare to step out of your so-called 'comfort' zone or area of safety. It is far better to look within yourself for the answers.

Do you trust yourself enough to try something new? Are you excited about what you could do or become? Are you willing to be open? Are you willing to be spontaneous and fun? Are you willing to risk being yourself?

The answer to any job-related issue is to look within yourself. Yes, sure, it is tempting to look externally and to change the external factors but these changes will offer you only temporary relief. Long-term job satisfaction is about taking yourself up higher and higher and becoming more centred on positive emotions and responses, such as being and showing love, compassion and trust within the working environment. It is about giving of yourself, accepting yourself and others, at all times.

On your journey of self-development there will always be the temptation to change job, especially if you spot an advertisement for your dream job. Stop and ask yourself, 'What is the benefit of this job or role?' 'How will I grow or develop by accepting it?' 'How will I stop developing if I accept it?' Then and only then can you make the decision that is best for you, for there is every chance that this new job will turn out like all the rest. If you are meant to have this job, it'll crop up again either in the same or a different way, when you are really ready to excel at it.

So a dream job will never be handed to you on a plate. You are going to have to work to achieve it. Sorry but there are no free prizes, no cheap gains and no quick fixes. The price you will have to pay to get a 'great job' has to be paid for in advance, just like everything else you buy. The cost is normally in terms of what you may have to sacrifice along the way in order to spark up your job and career. You may have to let that so-called dream job go by, or give up some of your leisure time doing the exercises or learning some new skills. The point is, you need to decide beforehand just how much you are willing to pay in time and resources in order to focus and work towards creating the job of your dreams.

Have you estimated the price you are willing to pay for it? Even though most people actually resist the thought of having to pay a price, they are frequently shocked to see just how small it is in relation to the real gain – the benefit of feeling good about their job most, if not all, of the time.

Another really important benefit is that knowing how much you are willing to pay up-front will help you to prepare yourself in terms of energy, resolve and commitment to achieve it. It will also help you to value the benefit later on, in terms of how far you have come and the effort you have expended. Trust that by creating and investing in the 'search for fulfilment' it will be a far better investment than just merely changing job for the sake of it, because what is your dream job now may not be what you are looking for in terms of ultimate satisfaction. Reserve judgment if you can, until you have completed all the exercises on yourself.

Take time out

The second way to escape the negative feelings about work is to take time out. As your work becomes more demanding or pressurised, do you take time out? Time out may be in the form of holiday, illness or even a few 'stress' days here and there. Voluntary absence is still by far the biggest reason for time off and as a result it causes the biggest headache and inconvenience for companies.

Until this becomes a habit or a real nuisance it is rarely tackled by the company, for it is generally recognised that if a few stress days here and there keep the employee on track, then so be it. However, for others the luxury of sneaking days off is not possible because redundancy gives them as many days as they would like to think things through! So beware! Your absence may be being noted in terms of your commitment to the company.

Plenty of other people when faced with the need to 'spark up' their job think that perhaps they should jack their job in, to actually give the whole spark question plenty of attention and focus. Do you feel this way? It is better, however, to think things through over a period of time rather than rushing at it. Time can be used more constructively and positively when there is no pressure to attain or achieve results rather than when your back is firmly against the wall with the bank manager, mortgage lender and credit card companies breathing down your neck.

Brace yourself; finding 'job fulfilment' isn't about doing it today and realising it tomorrow. It is about acceptance, growth and development. If you have already spent time working on yourself then your route to job fulfilment may be quicker than for someone who is new to searching within themself to discover the real answers to the job issue. But how long it takes you will depend upon how much time and effort you invest in the concept. Whereas some will achieve it in six weeks, others may take six months or even six years. Far more important than the time concept is the concept of responsibility. The actual fact that you have taken control of your career and that you are now managing it.

Dreams

The third way to escape from the pain cycle is to enter a type of dream or fantasy state. Is this your form of pain relief? Do you choose to make things feel better by separating yourself from the pain and by imagining and thinking about the day when fate will intervene and save you from your current situation? Do you think about winning the lottery, winning on a scratch card or the bingo or perhaps winning a load of money from a competition, or inheriting a large sum of money from a long-lost friend or relative? Do you plan what you would do with all this money down to the last detail, such as the type of house you'd have, the car you'd drive, the clothes you'd buy or the types of holidays you'd take? Do these dreams make you feel better but perhaps worse as well because nothing actually changes?

Dreams, fantasies and aspirations are brilliant. They make the unbearable seem slightly more bearable and they help you to detach yourself from the situation. Dreams act as a trigger to change but they have to be actioned.

Are your dreams and fantasies protecting you? To explain this in more detail: it means that even though you may have a negative thought or dream about something, it doesn't necessarily have to materialise. Likewise if you have a positive, powerful and wonderful thought and dream, it too doesn't necessarily have to arise either. The reason for this is that you have to manage and action your positive thoughts. Is it time therefore to action some of your dreams?

Your freedom to choose your thoughts is ultimately in your hands. Your thoughts are unique to you and no one else can get inside your head and experience what you experience. When you choose to manage your thoughts then you can choose to determine things like your feelings and how you respond and act in a given situation. It does, however, require effort and practice and will need to be worked at gradually and on an on-going basis.

The positive fact is that managing your thoughts helps to give you that sense of choice. You can choose to get frustrated with the system, blame it on luck or fate or you can choose to change your thinking altogether and decide to make it happen.

Making choices has to be developed and worked upon and the more positive decisions you make, the easier it'll become. The risk involved in making choices is not so much the risk of making a 'wrong' choice but the actual risk of making a 'right' choice. You are worth more and therefore could offer more to the work world.

Now is the time to get started. It is also time to face the truth, to feel the feelings of vulnerability and to concentrate on what you want to become. You have been waiting a long time for this moment and all you need to do now is to really start to work upon yourself, the new you, and develop aspects of yourself to bring about a new focus towards your work. A focus that enables you to arrive at a point of celebration about the process of work. First, it is a celebration about you because you are qualified, able, gifted and talented enough to make a worthwhile contribution. Second, it is a celebration about being in a position to do this at work and be well-paid for your contribution as well. It is about 'releasing' all of you so that you operate out of *love* rather than out of duty, obligation, fear and/or habit. By becoming more 'loving' in your interactions, work will become easier and easier for you to do and thereby to enjoy. Remember it starts with you, and as you do and become more loving your message will go out into the work world.

It is a simple and easy process and because of this it often gets ignored or overlooked. Give yourself the opportunity of being more loving towards others today. Let's get started *now!*

Step Two –
Releasing Yourself
from the Pain Cycle

This chapter is all about releasing yourself from the pain cycle and allowing your 'pain' to become your greatest incentive to change and/or improve. With the focus now on your 'self-development', it is possible to find new ways to give more to your job and workplace.

Release, however, is all about letting go of outdated ways or thoughts and not being attached to the end result or outcome. For attachment places too much emphasis on controlling, defending or protecting things, rather than allowing things to evolve and develop over time. By going with the flow or to some extent stepping into the new or unknown, you will begin to place more emphasis on trusting yourself. By listening to and responding to your thoughts, needs and feelings, you can then begin to follow a job path that is in-line with your newly formed beliefs, ideas and capabilities. Be aware, though, that there may be a time delay before you feel more ecstatic about your job. For example, some people experience numbness, or just quietness. They know they are no longer feeling negative but they also know that they are not quite there in terms of pleasure.

At this time, it'll take a lot of determination to resist your own temptation to give up working upon yourself or to question whether the whole self-development process is actually making the required difference. For although it is a simple and relatively straightforward process, it does require commitment to continue to work on yourself to see the 'full' results. Are you prepared to make that commitment to yourself, your job and ultimately your employer? The payback is there for the taking as long as you stick at it, and perhaps even come back to the programme from time to time. What actions do you need to take in order to release yourself from the pain cycle?

Action 1 –
Drop your controlling behaviour

Behaviour can be used to control, manage or manipulate a situation or person at work. 'Controlling' behaviour is behaviour that forces, convinces or entices another person to 'give in' to the individual using the behaviour. Controlling behaviour is usually a sign that an individual feels powerless, resistant or unaware of its short-term benefits and gains. There are four common forms of controlling behaviour and each one will be described in turn.

'Unlucky me' behaviour

This behaviour involves the individual gaining sympathy, support and/or help by moaning or groaning to others about a person or situation. 'Unlucky me' phrases are things like:

- If only I could have such and such.
- How nice it would be for me to have that.
- You're luckier than me.

- You have more than me.
- Life is harder for me.

'Cold' behaviour

This behaviour involves the individual simply becoming aloof or ignoring others in order to get the attention back onto themself because the other person is worried or concerned. This behaviour creates feelings of guilt, shame or helplessness in others and encourages them to lure the 'cold' person out of their mood.

'Questioner' behaviour

This behaviour is a direct, aggressive and intimidating approach. It involves confronting someone with questions in order to reveal the truth or to force action. For example, the questioner might ask another person:

- Why did you do that?
- Why didn't you help?
- Why did you say that?
- Why do you feel that?

'I'm the best' behaviour

This behaviour involves the individual feeling the need to prove their expertise and prowess for their ideas, actions, projects, role, beliefs, plans, performance, results and achievements to others.

All of these behaviours act as a smokescreen for the underlying need inside you. Needs is a big topic and can easily be dismissed or ignored because there is a tendency to hide needs away at work. If you aren't satisfying your needs, they'll keep cropping up until you look at them and sort them out.

Drop your controlling behaviour by beginning to acknowledge and recognise your needs. For example, instead of playing a 'unlucky me', you can begin to talk to others in terms of what you need from them, or would like to see happen. Start to get comfortable about acknowledging and responding to your own very important needs.

What are your needs at the moment? How often do you re-evaluate your needs – monthly, six-monthly or hardly ever? How well is your work satisfying your current needs? If you have a bad day at work, are you aware of what need wasn't satisfied? How are you going to remedy the situation? Are you comfortable about talking about your needs? Common needs are listed on pages 32–3. Change is about working upon what 'need' you aren't satisfying. Controlling behaviour has a limited shelf-life and invites you to receive the same behaviour from others in return. It can very easily lure you into the illusion that everyone else has to change rather than you!

It is worth pointing out that you may not notice your controlling behaviour initially. It is often only when you start looking at yourself that you draw people towards you who have similar issues to solve in order to help you 'see' your issue more clearly. So what you notice in others is key to your change process. For example, you may notice people who are using the 'cold' drama a lot. How do you react when you see others using their dramas? It is essential that if you notice others adopting a drama that you too don't get hooked into it or tempted to use your dramas.

To get the other person to drop their drama, you need to focus on the person and quite simply name the drama that the person is using or ask the person what they need within the given situation. You may discover that people are so unused to people asking them directly what they need that they might give you a blank or an unusual look. This is just a sign that you are treating the person differently, so carry on with the same question but phrased in a different way such as, 'What would help you in these circumstances?' Dig deep and begin to recognise and satisfy your own needs and help others to focus on their needs too.

Remember that if you look to others to satisfy your needs by adopting any of the above behaviours you are giving your power away. Power that is rightfully yours, so harness your needs and use your power wisely.

Action 2 – Drop the 'but' word

The biggest thing that will keep you in the pain cycle is the 'but' word. 'But' is such a powerful word, as it allows you to discount everything you say before it. For example,

- I agree with everything in principle *but* will it work for me?
- I accept it *but* have I got the time?
- I want to break the cycle *but* is there an easier way?

'But' allows you to stop thinking about action and to focus and dwell on your current situation again, thereby remaining firmly in the pain cycle. To break this habit try to replace the 'but' word with '*and*'. Change any questions about the process into positive factual statements. These statements then allow you to get used to the fact that you need to take positive action.

Action 3 – Take full responsibility for yourself

Taking responsibility is all about accepting that you own the problem and therefore can create the solution too. It is about turning your question 'Is this it?' around to 'Yes, this is it.' What this means is that instead of questioning everything or creating conditions for your happiness you need to start to talk and think more positively. For example, move from negative thoughts to factual thoughts.

- From 'I need to earn a bigger salary in order to be happy' to '*I earn this at the moment and have the potential to earn more.*'
- From 'I need to have a nicer boss' to '*I have a tricky boss right now and I deserve to find a boss who suits me better.*'

- From 'I need people to be more friendly to me' to '*I have people around me who do respond to me.*'

The focus is on the right-here-and-now. In effect, it is on the present. You must try to stop thinking too hard about your job and quantifying your circumstances. Begin to get to a point where you can accept things as they are, and then the heat and frustration is taken out of the situation and your natural state becomes one of acceptance. Acceptance means that you can begin to see the 'truth' in all situations, what is real and ultimately what needs changing. Acceptance is all about the present and creating stability, peace and calm within you. It stops that constant yearning and 'What if . . . ?' feeling and it also allows you to get used to embracing things as they are right now. So, sure, a healthy bank balance would be more preferable to an unhealthy bank balance but as you know already it isn't going to change overnight and forcing your boss to pay you more could have dire consequences. The trick is to accept things as they are right now and stop trying to 'control' things. There may be many, many aspects of your work life or job that you don't like but work on yourself before you dash out to try to change things quickly.

Action 4 – Appreciate the present

Whatever you focus upon grows in importance and you then attract more of it into your work life. Heavy and negative thoughts create negative experiences for you. To change from a negative to a positive state you have to create the conditions in which your enthusiasm for your job can grow. You need therefore to begin to appreciate your current circumstances. There are many things that you can be grateful for that you are currently overlooking.

Acknowledge everything that is either good for you or important to you, in your present job. Below is an example for you to have a look at and then have a go yourself. Try to fill in five things about your work that you value no matter how dire your current circumstances. Have a go and see whether you can surprise yourself!

Example

A school teacher is midway through a term and is feeling that the weeks aren't going quickly enough and that the pay cheque isn't stretching far enough.

1 I value my job because *I am constantly being challenged to keep myself up-to-date.*
2 I value my job because *I get the opportunity to see whether my pupils have enjoyed their lessons or not.*
3 I value my job because *I have the opportunity to work with fresh, young and lively people who encourage me to be the same.*
4 I value my job because *I enjoy training and imparting technical information to others in a clear, precise and informative way.*
5 I value my job because *I enjoy the perks of the job such as long holidays, school trips, field trips, trips abroad, weekends off and short working days.*

Your turn now

1 I value my job because

2 I value my job because

3 I value my job because

4 I value my job because

5 I value my job because

Positive, inspiring thoughts create positive, inspiring experiences. As you begin to value yourself, others and your job more, you will receive more public and verbal recognition of your worth in return.

By appreciating things you will be able to create more of the things that you like and are good at. What are you good at? Isn't it time you started to recognise your own value and contribution?

Action 5 – Drop the serious attitude

Stop all the frenzy of your activity within your day-to-day job. Being frantic and constantly busy means that you question yourself. Do you ask yourself a lot of questions? For example, 'Where did I put that?' 'Where is that report?' 'When do I have to do that by?' 'What happens if I don't make the deadline?' 'Will that be a popular decision?' Frantic questioning helps to keep you constantly checking up on yourself and it keeps you uptight, serious and constantly busy. Does this feel like you? Do you struggle to remember what you've done in the day but you know that you've been on the go all the time? Rushing all day helps to keep you focusing on the trivia and negative things that can determine whether or not your day was good or bad.

To move away from this, make use of the 'when' question. The 'when' question helps take away the decision bit and allows you to focus on the end result and the pleasure thoughts that the end result will create. For example, 'When am I going to stop?' 'When am I going to relax?' 'When am I going to have a really good laugh?' 'When will that report be finished?'

Moving away from all that intellectual thinking and seriousness and allowing yourself to get back into becoming more light-hearted, funny, happy, contented and calm will help you to become a freer, more liberated person. What is more important: the rules and regulations, or being honest with yourself? Honesty means that there is no image for you to keep up, so there is no explaining, excuses or pretence to do. Honesty is about you becoming a relaxed, honest and happy worker who doesn't take themself too seriously. Work isn't about being serious, so strive for satisfaction and honesty. Below is some space for you to pick out five instances where perhaps you were too serious about your work and now is the time to make amends for your own and other people's benefit. Fill in the examples in the knowledge that next time you'll find it easier to behave or respond in a more favourable way. Have a go and remember, don't take the exercise too seriously. It is not about beating yourself up or feeling bad about the past; it is about working out ways to be more light-hearted. Have a go.

1 I was too serious at work when

Next time I will

2 I was too serious at work when

Next time I will

3 I was too serious at work when

Next time I will

4 I was too serious at work when

Next time I will

5 I was too serious at work when

Next time I will

Do you feel lighter now? Self-reflection and self-analysis are great career management tools for they help you to break the patterns of the past. This stops you from hiding your true worth and enables you to forgive yourself. Forgiveness is crucial to your self-development process as it means that you will never become stuck in negative ways or negative habits. It enables you to constantly be looking for ways to extend yourself. Hence, self-reflection and self-analysis help you to reclaim your power and have an incentive to improve your work situation.

Did you complete the questions? If you did, great. If you didn't complete the questions, did you feel that on some level you would be admitting your mistakes? Or perhaps as if you were making a list of people you had wronged, yourself included? Acceptance isn't about beating yourself up, it is about making amends. Allow yourself to change. Changing aspects of your approach to work allows you to become more 'professional' and powerful as a person and enables you to make a difference to the work environment. Power means asking yourself, 'What do I have to offer here?' 'What can I do to help and when am I going to start?' Therefore, go beyond the duties of your job description and offer more. Respond before you are asked and give rather than criticise.

Action 6 – Listen and respond to your wake-up calls

Wake-up calls help take you from the pain cycle and into the pleasure cycle. Your job-related wake-up calls tell you what you need to learn and allow you to decide whether you respond to that invitation. Many people have described the effect of wake-up calls as recovering from the dead or the humdrum of work. A wake-up call can help a person to realise that work can be different and offers the person an insight into their new work vision or an area of work that needs their attention.

What you take from this wake-up section will depend upon how much you believe or start to believe in the 'purpose of your working life'. Do you believe in fate? Do you believe that you are on this planet to do a specific job, task or type of work? Whatever your beliefs, thoughts or ideas on the subject, take the time to consider any wake-up calls you may have had or are having. They will certainly help guide you in your job decisions. Let's take a closer look at wake-up calls in more detail. Examples of typical wake-up calls are as follows:

- The loss of someone close to you, which changes your focus about work.
- An article about the type of work that does interest you.
- A period of sickness or illness during which you consider doing something more worthwhile, purposeful or different.
- A glimpse of what you really want by witnessing it in others.
- A realisation that you are dissatisfied with your work day after day, week after week.
- A recurring dream about work or the type of work that would suit you.
- A television programme, film or video that arouses important feelings, ideas or thoughts.
- People telling you the same thing in different ways.
- The birth of a child, which changes your focus about work.
- A speeding fine or a parking ticket, hinting that you are speeding through your life.
- Redundancy or the loss of your job, forcing you to do something about your circumstances.

However it presents itself, the wake-up call has a message for you – the message that your work life needs to be redirected or changed in some way.

It is worth pointing out here that people are often so busy and entrenched in their everyday activities and routines that they initially don't hear their wake-up calls. Hence it is important to have silence in your job and to reduce the amount of automatic activity. Most wake-up calls start very gently and quietly. They are almost a 'whisper' in your head. Thus, it can be easy to miss them. Initially the calls may be newspaper clips, news items, passing conversations with strangers and then the significance of them can be missed. Why? Because perhaps you were flicking through the newspaper on your way to work, or parking the car while the news was on or not really paying attention to what the stranger was saying?

So many wake-up calls get missed because people are too busy to hear them or they don't regard themselves as special enough to receive one. Yes, it is true that many people feel: 'Not me, surely. I mean, I couldn't possibly do that, be that or do that justice. No, this doesn't refer to me – Who? Me? No, there must be someone else who is more talented, qualified and able than I am, so who shall I talk to about this?'

It is not always easy to think in terms of how special, wonderful or worthy you are. In fact, many people can readily recount all the people who haven't thought that much of them; perhaps it was their old boss, their ex-colleague or departmental head. In fact your wake-up calls are preparing you to believe and accept that you are worth so much more. They are telling you loud and clear that you could and need to change. However, unless you respond to the calls, resistance can set in. Resistance is the thing which often stops you from changing and keeps you firmly in your comfort zone – the bit you know, understand and feel comfortable with. While you resist, though, you are simply putting off the inevitable. How do you resist things? Listed below are many forms of resistance. Tick or circle the ones you use:

- Being late
- Not listening
- Talking too much

- Forgetting things
- Apologising for things
- Avoiding things
- Making deliberate mistakes
- Justifying your position
- Protecting yourself
- Getting angry or aggressive
- Dropping things
- Pretending to be tired
- Getting up and leaving the room
- Making excuses
- Or denying things.

Initially resistance tactics work; if you continue to use them that forces the wake-up calls to become louder and louder and perhaps even more dramatic. Then, the wake-up call forces you to stop, listen and look at the situation with perhaps more 'vulnerable' or fresh eyes.

Are you so entrenched in your duties, jobs and tasks that you fail to actually see the bigger, better picture? Hence the use of the phrase, 'wake-up call'. Are you asleep at work – asleep to the new opportunities and choices that lie ahead? When a 'sleep' state pervades, the new, the different and the positive can be perceived as a threat, scary or maybe even too good to be true. Hence the wake-up call for a person in the 'sleep' state might be regarded as odd, peculiar, crazy, perhaps even as a bit 'religious', or simply as dangerous. Those who choose to react negatively to the wake-up call may choose to pretend it is not happening, deny it and push it to the back of their mind. Millions of people remain 'asleep' as long as they can (hopefully through to retirement and beyond). However, the beauty of wake-up calls is that they will keep coming and normally with greater and greater intensity.

Where does this lead you? Wake-up calls will continue to happen because the underlying message is that 'You are far more than you think you are and you will have as many chances as you need at the message being relayed to you, until you get it!'

How do people respond to their wake-up calls? Some people wait and wait, not responding to the call until such time as they can no longer ignore it, whereas others simply get a whiff of a message and they respond. They don't even ask themselves, 'Why me? I'm too old or too young.' They are merely delighted to be given an opportunity to do something new, different and worthwhile even if they don't know where it will lead them in the future. What drives them is the wake-up call itself.

Think now about your life and list below anything that you might regard as a wake-up call. If you can't think of anything right now, take the time to refer back to this section as the thoughts come up later on.

My wake-up calls

1 My wake-up call consisted of

2 I received a wake-up call when I heard

3 I had a wake-up call when I saw

4 However painful it is for me to admit, I had a wake-up call when

5 I have a huge desire to do something when I hear, see or feel

6 I am so grateful that I had a wake-up call along the lines of

7 I really admire _____ and in seeing this person it wakes
   up a part of me because

Receiving wake-up calls is a sign that you need to make some changes. Do you get caught up in the emotion around the wake-up call itself? Emotions such as, 'How could this have happened?' 'This is difficult', 'Why me?' 'Why is this happening to me?' 'Why do I have to suffer?' 'I don't deserve this.' Or do you use a wake-up call as a sign that something is about to change in your working life and that 'something' is in your best interests?

It is too tempting to go down the route of self-pity and self-indulgence and to expect someone else to haul you out or make it all better for you. Yes, it is so much more empowering and wonderful to trust that this wake-up call has happened for a reason and it is for you to have the confidence to believe that you are the person to do something about it. It is time for you to help, respond and make that difference now. The power questions later on in this chapter will help you make sure that you don't let the situation, person or comment 'get to you' and they will enable you to stay in the present and to respond positively to the wake-up call.

So, with any wake-up call, stop, listen and reflect for a while. It may be that you need to change your profession, field of work

or direction of work. Or as is more likely, it may mean that you
need to develop further personal skills. Ask yourself, 'Do I need
to make amends anywhere?' 'Do I need to focus on worthiness?'
It is important to recognise where you are within your career
development and to notice the 'unseen' and 'unnoticed' bits so
that you can be active in your development. Thus, be aware of
your wake-up calls, write them down in future and note their
significance to your development, as they are there to guide
you forward and to help you develop your resilience, qualities,
confidence, trust and sense of self-belief. They are your 'gifts'
and can take you further and further up the career ladder or
along your career path.

Action 7 – Reassess your beliefs
about your job or work

The action you take *now* is to do with reassessing your opinions
or beliefs about work. For it is only by taking a good, close look at
those 'old friends' of yours that you can really decide whether your
beliefs are helping or hindering you in the pain or pleasure cycle.
In simple terms, it is only your beliefs about work that determine
whether you are either happy or unhappy about your job or career-
to-date.

Beliefs are very powerful things. They can do many of the
following:

* Make you feel happy or sad
* Convince you that you are rich or poor
* Make you feel that you are successful or unsuccessful
* Convince you that you are powerful or weak
* Make you feel popular or unpopular
* Convince you that you have potential or limited opportunity
* Make you feel that you can or can't have the job you desire.

Beliefs about work are a fact of life and, yes, you need them in order to thrive. The positive thing about beliefs is that they help you determine what is right and wrong, what is good or bad, who is similar to or different from you. They can help you to unravel many of the complexities of work. Beliefs can, on the other hand, be a real hindrance too because they can get in the way and stop you from looking at yourself. For you can believe that you don't need to improve. Is this the case for you?

The development of your own belief system is predominantly tribal. You learnt a lot about your beliefs about work from your family and during your early years. These beliefs about work encourage you to follow or accept certain work attitudes, ethics or responsibilities. As a result, they help you to work with others in a smooth and effective manner, as you are likely to choose to work with others who share similar beliefs about work to you. Many of these beliefs are based upon rules and regulations that you feel need to apply and which, to some extent, attract you into your chosen job, profession or career in the first place.

Thus, beliefs become very much apart of who and what you are and what you choose to do, and how you choose to behave and respond to others. Sometimes, however, your present beliefs about work, your place of work and the people that you come into contact with are hindering you. Your beliefs about work may be:

- Old-fashioned
- Holding you back
- Outdated
- Inappropriate
- Too negative
- Interfering with your career development
- Or not based upon truth.

People who work closely together tend to hold similar beliefs about the same types of issues. Hence the status quo is kept intact and even if one person spots a difference of opinion or belief it tends to be common practice to explain it away. For no one wants to challenge the group because busy lives force people to make instant and quick decisions that reject the belief rather than look at it. Trouble occurs only when another person disagrees with, challenges or criticises a particular individual's belief system. If you are challenged on your beliefs, then how do you feel?

- Hurt
- Upset
- Annoyed
- Cross
- Shamed
- Or picked upon.

If your beliefs are challenged do you immediately find another tribal member to console, support, comfort or agree with you? Do you both agree that the challenger is at fault? Finding a supporter rather than looking at your beliefs runs the risk of stopping your development job-wise.

What is required is for you to take the time and effort to go inside yourself and to look at and question your beliefs. When you take the time, you will always discover something to develop and this something is just beyond where you are at the moment. So the process involves detaching yourself from the importance of your belief and looking at it again with fresh eyes. Does your belief really serve your best interests? Is this belief the best choice you could make or is there a better belief you could have?

Your belief system has probably been with you for most if not all of your working life, and it can be a bit unnerving to look at it. Do you feel alone, unsure of yourself or a bit doubtful? Or do you feel vulnerable? Feelings of vulnerability can be aroused when the belief system is reassessed because there may be fewer beliefs now than in the past to cling on to. Thus, the vulnerability that you actually feel allows you the opportunity to formulate and create supportive, flexible and positive beliefs, on an on-going basis. It forces you to develop and not to get too comfortable because as soon as you do get comfortable, you can be tempted to stop developing further.

The good news, as always, is that vulnerability is a perfectly normal and natural part of the change process, because in order to move forward you have to let go of the old and release the 'control' to some extent. This way of thinking can delude you into believing that you have:

- Got it right
- Got it wrong
- Got it under control.

When you can accept this, a huge shift will take place in your consciousness. This shift involves a movement from *control* to *trust*. The trust lies deep within you and will allow you to:

- Tap into the present moment
- See things as they really are
- Drop all control tactics
- Know everything is working out for the best
- And finally to step out of your old ways and to begin to move forward in the best way for you.

What beliefs do you have about your job and work?

Your beliefs

Much of the way you choose to think *now* about work and its opportunities for you depends upon how you were raised and what you learnt about work from your family. What did you learn? For many it was that the man's job or career was the most important one. For example, the man's job was of highest importance and as a result all the focus and attention was on him and his work. He was the main breadwinner, so he was regarded as having and was given pride of place in the family. Maybe he talked about his work at home in terms of what he was doing, planning and achieving or maybe he chose not to talk about his work at all. Very often work was just something that took place between 9 a.m. and 5 p.m., Monday to Friday. Whatever the man's work, it was rare for men to think or even remotely consider things like taking time out of work to retrain, travel the world or simply to have a well-earned break. Work was and still is for many something they do for 40 or 50 years. The lucky ones were seen as those who managed to avoid being laid off at any time. If they did, their first priority was to pull themselves up and get back into work as soon as they could. Job fulfilment wasn't something they considered of primary importance and if they did enjoy their job it was a *bonus*.

What did you learn about work for women? Was it that work was something they didn't have to worry themselves about? They were 'taken care' of by their men and their role was to keep house, look after their husband, raise the children and, if they really wanted it, maybe have a part-time, voluntary or perhaps an evening job or a career once the children were grown up. In the past there was a big stigma around women working. Men felt proud they could provide for their family and women had a very different role.

Your parents or grandparents may have been very different but a key message from previous generations concerning work was that if everyone did their bit, things would continue to prosper and the bills would be paid – there was little mention of enjoyment.

Whatever message you learnt from your upbringing, whether it is the same as or different from the above, it will have helped you to initially formalise and decide what was appropriate in career terms for you. Have you chosen to follow suit in relation to your role models or have you chosen to do something completely different? How much have your elders influenced your job decisions?

Beliefs about work may be weak or strong in terms of what you can or can't do, in relation to work. Some examples of work beliefs are listed below:

- Unless you've made it by 40 your chances of doing it are over.
- You have to travel in order to be regarded as a success.
- You have to work for a big company.
- You have to have a professional training and qualification in order to get on.
- You have to behave in a certain way in order to be successful.
- A woman can't have a family and work and do both properly.
- You can't change job too often.
- You have to 'get to the top' before you can have fun.
- You have to do things in a certain way.
- You have to enter the family firm or family profession.
- Only men can be really successful.
- Only women can be really successful!

All of these beliefs are limiting beliefs and they *stop* the person who holds them from developing fully. Work is not really about so many extremes – it is just your opinions about work that create the limitations to your career development. Search out any of your beliefs that are limiting your progress in any way and replace them with more constructive beliefs, and your attitude and performance have the potential to dramatically improve.

Listed below are a number of questions, which are intended to help you write down your beliefs about work. The questions have been designed to help you identify and examine which beliefs you'll keep and which ones you'll discard. This will enable you to recognise which beliefs are holding you back and which beliefs may need to be developed further. (You can do this exercise with any issue that you are working on. Just replace the word 'work' with the word of your choice. Hence you may want to replace 'work' with words such as boss, friends, salaries, holidays, computers, relationships. You can use this exercise to improve other areas of your work life. Use this exercise when you are struggling to resolve any work issue.)

Your beliefs about work

1 What beliefs about work have you inherited from your male role model?

2 What beliefs about work have you inherited from your female role model?

3 What beliefs about work have you inherited from your brother, sister or cousins?

4 What beliefs about work have you created as a result of your first job/education?

5 What beliefs about work have you created as a result of your earning capacity?

6 What beliefs about work have you created as a result of your colleagues' attitudes?

7 What beliefs about work have you created as a result of your environment?

8 What beliefs about work did you have as a child?

9 How have your beliefs changed as a result of your work experiences?

So, what did you discover about yourself and your inherited beliefs? Now go back over your belief answers and see whether your beliefs are mostly negative or mostly positive. With regard to your negative beliefs, ask yourself whether you want to rid yourself of this belief forever, in which case do, or rephrase it and make it into a new positive seedling belief. A seedling belief is a belief that needs to be repeated over and over in your mind in order to emerge as a truly believable belief. So, sure, your immediate reaction may be, 'I don't believe that!' But then ask yourself, 'Am I willing to work on it in order to believe it?'

Realise that as you change your beliefs, so your feelings change and this in turn will change your actions and your future too. Although you may feel uncomfortable about affirming: 'I am successful at whatever I choose to focus on', 'Everything I do is a success' and 'I deserve to be successful', continue at it and notice how you and others respond. Surround yourself with successful, positive people and realise that you can turn your destiny around if you are committed. Realise that removing and shedding the 'bad' stuff in terms of beliefs will help you to keep your focus on the pleasure bit, rather than the struggle bit. Let the old beliefs go and then you will discover that you are now lighter, fresher and freer to experience the present more fully and fulfil your mission to achieve that sense of purpose within your daily work.

Action 8 – Ask yourself power questions

This has been left to last because it is the most important action of all. Power questions help you to feel in control, and able to deal *now* with your work issues. No matter where you are or what you are doing at present, you want 'more' from your job and your working life. Whether or not you achieve this depends upon how well you manage your painful and pleasurable experiences. If you don't manage your experiences you will find that your experiences will manage you.

Everything you do at work depends upon whether you view it as a painful experience or a pleasurable experience. Are there things at work that you aren't doing that you know you should be doing? Everything that you do at work, you do for a reason and this reason is based upon your need to gain either pleasure or your need to avoid pain. Although you may regard this as an oversimplification, everything you do is based upon what you link pain or pleasure to. Why aren't you doing certain things at work? Quite simply it is because you have linked pain to these experiences. However, the experiences themselves don't actually cause you pain, just as in the same way your pleasurable experiences don't actually create pleasure. Thus, it is only your perception of the experience that labels it as either a good or a bad experience. In short, you are not driven by reality but what you determine as being 'real' for you.

How do you change? How do you move forward? The first step is to be aware of what you link pleasure to. If something isn't happening at work ask yourself, 'Do I view this as a pleasure or a painful experience?' 'What have I closed off to?' 'What do I need to link pleasure to, in order to take action?' You also need to start to become aware of whether your links are positive or negative. For example, just say in the past you had a horrible female boss. You may have linked pain to *all* female bosses and therefore this may be limiting your current choices. So ask yourself, 'What is the cause of my pain?' In the same way, perhaps in the past you had an awful experience when you made a speech in public; you may have decided never to do it again, therefore closing yourself off to opportunities. Therefore, you have to override your conditioning and work out what would be pleasurable about having a female boss or speaking in public.

The second step is to condition yourself to long-term pleasure. For in order to move forward and achieve success you have to go through 'your' perception of the 'short-term pain'. Focus on the possibility of the pain of 'not taking action'. 'What will happen if you don't do what you ought to be doing?' 'What will you miss out on as a result?' Thus, begin to focus on the pain of not taking action rather than the pleasure of avoiding taking action. Hence your behaviour will change instantly.

The third step is to turn your questions into power questions. Instead of focusing on the pain, focus on the pleasure by asking yourself:

- How am I responsible for this situation?
- What is false about what I have focused upon to date?
- When can I get started and take action?
- How could I help myself create more positive associations of pleasure?

See how effective this process is by using it to bring about more pleasurable experiences for yourself. Manage the situation rather than allowing the situation to manage you.

You have had the opportunity to reflect upon a lot here in this chapter and the key question is: How do you actually feel now? Circle or tick the most appropriate words.

- Lighter
- More energised
- Buzzy
- Happier
- More up-beat
- Keen
- Sparkier
- More excited
- Ready

The following chapters are all about your journey towards pleasure and spark. There is a questionnaire and a bit of daily work for you to do in order to make any adjustments or amendments to yourself, your attitude, behaviour or performance. If you don't want to do this work just ask yourself, 'What am I associating with pain here?' and 'How can I turn this into a pleasurable experience?'

Step Three – The Creative Cycle

The creative cycle is about creating 'more' in terms of personal skills and qualities. The action you take in a job is directly related and interlinked with your energy supply. This cycle is a two-stage process. The first process involves completing the self-development questionnaire and thereby discovering your personal strengths and qualities, and gaining an insight about your energy supply, in terms of how you are allowing it to be depleted.

The second part of the process is all about developing ways to create more energy, which you will need if you are committed to giving 'more of' yourself to your job. The diagram opposite clearly highlights the various stages of the creative cycle.

Your enthusiasm about your job is directly related to your energy supply. If work is a struggle, then your energy will be low and you may find yourself feeling tired, stressed or empty a lot of the time. If work is purposeful, exciting, meaningful, rewarding and is benefiting you and others then your energy is likely to be high most of the time.

Energy, like everything else, has to be worked upon in order to keep it consistent and high. People who have fulfilling jobs tend

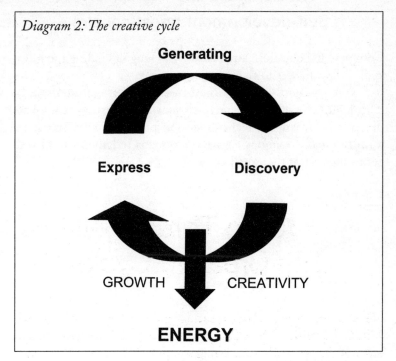

Diagram 2: The creative cycle

Generating

Express   **Discovery**

GROWTH   CREATIVITY

ENERGY

to have bags of energy and their energy is consistently high, whether they are facing a crisis or celebration, whether they have won or lost a contract, or whether it is five o'clock in the morning or 11 o'clock at night. Their secret isn't that they have found a way to supercharge their batteries but that they take responsibility for their energy and they monitor and build their energy throughout the day.

As you become more self-aware and self-reflective your energy will increase, for energy relates to lightness and, as you build, restock and stop your energy draining, you'll reach greater and greater levels of perfection and performance, and you'll feel lighter. Thus you'll find it easier and more rewarding to give of yourself. As your energy begins to balance and establish a comfortable level within your body, if and when it drops, it'll take less effort and work to top it up – because you have a blip in your energy supply rather than a depletion in it.

Self-development questionnaire

Complete the questionnaire below by ticking or circling the most appropriate answer to the question.

Before you start, it is important to say, be gentle on yourself. If it brings up a lot of issues or anguish do what you can and complete the exercise when you feel calmer and more relaxed. Try not to form too many opinions or make too many judgments until you get to the end of the exercise.

1 Anger

1. Do you use anger to get out of resolving a situation?   Frequently   Rarely   Never

2. Do you get angry with yourself?   Frequently   Rarely   Never

3. Do you get angry with others?   Frequently   Rarely   Never

4. Do you get angry about your background, education or parents?   Frequently   Rarely   Never

5. Do you feel angry towards your boss?   Frequently   Rarely   Never

6. Do you get angry with your tools, equipment or environment?   Frequently   Rarely   Never

7. Do you get angry about the lack of time?   Frequently   Rarely   Never

8	Do you get angry with the children, the animals or anyone or anything else?	Frequently	Rarely	Never
9	Do you get angry when you don't get your own way?	Frequently	Rarely	Never
10	Does change make you angry?	Frequently	Rarely	Never
11	Do you get angry with the government or authorities?	Frequently	Rarely	Never

2 Criticism

12	Do you use criticism to try to resolve things?	Frequently	Rarely	Never
13	Do you criticise yourself?	Frequently	Rarely	Never
14	Do you criticise your boss?	Frequently	Rarely	Never
15	Do you criticise other people's timekeeping abilities?	Frequently	Rarely	Never
16	Do you criticise the environment, lighting, noise, tools and equipment?	Frequently	Rarely	Never
17	Do you criticise your performance?	Frequently	Rarely	Never
18	Do you criticise other people's performance?	Frequently	Rarely	Never

19	Do you criticise other people's attitude or behaviour?	Frequently	Rarely	Never
20	Do you use criticism in order to make yourself feel or appear in a better light?	Frequently	Rarely	Never
21	Do you criticise anything else to take the focus off you?	Frequently	Rarely	Never
22	Do you criticise authorities or people in authority?	Frequently	Rarely	Never

3 Overcompromising/Pleasing

23	Do you put others before yourself?	Frequently	Rarely	Never
24	Do you give in easily?	Frequently	Rarely	Never
25	Do you keep quiet to avoid a fuss?	Frequently	Rarely	Never
26	Do you feel you could always do more?	Frequently	Rarely	Never
27	Do you feel that you don't count as a person?	Frequently	Rarely	Never
28	Do you think others will like you more if you give in?	Frequently	Rarely	Never
29	Do you step down in order to keep the peace?	Frequently	Rarely	Never

| 30 | Do you do things against your better judgment? | Frequently | Rarely | Never |

| 31 | Do you think about what might make others happy? | Frequently | Rarely | Never |

| 32 | Do you say '*No*'? | Frequently | Rarely | Never |

| 33 | Do you feel you don't really contribute as a person? | Frequently | Rarely | Never |

4 Revenge

| 34 | Do you think about getting your own back when something goes wrong or when someone accuses you of something? | Frequently | Rarely | Never |

| 35 | Do you try to go one better in order to get even? | Frequently | Rarely | Never |

| 36 | Do you think about the accusations after they have been said? | Frequently | Rarely | Never |

| 37 | Do you retaliate against other people's comments and suggestions? | Frequently | Rarely | Never |

| 38 | Do you try to rally people onto your side by telling them what you have been accused of? | Frequently | Rarely | Never |

39	Do you think nasty things about someone in order to make yourself feel better?	Frequently	Rarely	Never
40	Do you try to get back or to get even with the authorities?	Frequently	Rarely	Never
41	Do you spend time proving yourself to others?	Frequently	Rarely	Never
42	Do you ignore people who have accused you of something?	Frequently	Rarely	Never
43	Do you 'spoil' things in order to feel better yourself?	Frequently	Rarely	Never
44	Do you carry out your plans or try to set people up?	Frequently	Rarely	Never

5 Judgment

45	Do you judge yourself?	Frequently	Rarely	Never
46	Do you judge others?	Frequently	Rarely	Never
47	Do you think you know how others 'should' behave or treat others, within a situation?	Frequently	Rarely	Never
48	Do you jump to conclusions about things?	Frequently	Rarely	Never
49	Do you tell other people 'what to do'?	Frequently	Rarely	Never

50	Do you get to know people and how it is for them?	Frequently	Rarely Never
51	Do you fact-find and do your research?	Frequently	Rarely Never
52	Do you think you know why certain things happen?	Frequently	Rarely Never
53	Do you make assumptions about things?	Frequently	Rarely Never
54	Do you hear what you want to hear when someone is talking to you?	Frequently	Rarely Never
55	Do you think some people lack skills, capabilities and/or knowledge?	Frequently	Rarely Never

6 Regret

56	Do you think about 'what might have been'?	Frequently	Rarely Never
57	Do you think about how you could have done something better?	Frequently	Rarely Never
58	Do you wish you hadn't been so quick off the mark?	Frequently	Rarely Never
59	Do you ever wish you hadn't said or written something?	Frequently	Rarely Never

60	Do you wish you could be more understanding?	Frequently	Rarely	Never
61	Do you wish you could listen more?	Frequently	Rarely	Never
62	Do you wish you could make amends?	Frequently	Rarely	Never
63	Do you ever regret the way you've spent your time or conducted yourself in the past?	Frequently	Rarely	Never
64	Do you ever wish you hadn't been so foolish?	Frequently	Rarely	Never
65	Do you ever wish you could have managed a situation or handled a situation better?	Frequently	Rarely	Never
66	Do you ever wish you could have explained yourself better?	Frequently	Rarely	Never

7 Resentment

67	Do you ever feel, 'It is not fair'?	Frequently	Rarely	Never
68	Does it matter if others have more than you do?	Frequently	Rarely	Never
69	Are you happy with what you earn?	Frequently	Rarely	Never
70	Do you ever feel left out?	Frequently	Rarely	Never

71 Do you resent anything, anyone, even your partner?   Frequently   Rarely   Never

72 Do you ever fall out with people?   Frequently   Rarely   Never

73 Do you deliberately try to drain other people's enthusiasm?   Frequently   Rarely   Never

74 Do you resent the demands of the job?   Frequently   Rarely   Never

75 Do you resent the demands of the customers?   Frequently   Rarely   Never

76 Do you resent the unpaid effort you have to put into the job?   Frequently   Rarely   Never

77 Do you resent where you are within the organisation?   Frequently   Rarely   Never

78 Are you resentful if others don't recognise your valuable and worthy contribution?   Frequently   Rarely   Never

8 Control

79 Do you try to control yourself?   Frequently   Rarely   Never

80 Do you try to control what other people do?   Frequently   Rarely   Never

81 Do you try to control time?   Frequently   Rarely   Never

82	Do you try to control other people's emotions? – 'Don't feel that or say that'	Frequently	Rarely	Never
83	Do you try to control other people's behaviour? – 'Stop doing that, it is not allowed'.	Frequently	Rarely	Never
84	Are you ever tempted to think that you are 'perfect' or 'right'?	Frequently	Rarely	Never
85	Are you ever tempted to think that you 'know best'?	Frequently	Rarely	Never
86	Are you ever tempted to think that you no longer need to learn anything?	Frequently	Rarely	Never
87	Are you ever tempted to tell others how they could improve themselves?	Frequently	Rarely	Never
88	Are you ever tempted to think that you are more important, therefore you deserve to come first?	Frequently	Rarely	Never
89	Are you ever tempted to think that it isn't you who needs to change?	Frequently	Rarely	Never

9 Worry/Fear

90	Do you ever feel that it's not worth it?	Frequently	Rarely	Never

91	Do you ever think it is not going to work out or happen for you?	Frequently	Rarely	Never
92	Do you ever worry that people don't like you?	Frequently	Rarely	Never
93	Do you ever worry that you are not as good as others?	Frequently	Rarely	Never
94	Do you worry that you'll make a mistake?	Frequently	Rarely	Never
95	Do you worry about embarrassing yourself?	Frequently	Rarely	Never
96	Do you worry about your performance?	Frequently	Rarely	Never
97	Do you worry about the past?	Frequently	Rarely	Never
98	Do you worry about being ill?	Frequently	Rarely	Never
99	Do you worry about taking responsibility for things?	Frequently	Rarely	Never
100	Do you worry about your future?	Frequently	Rarely	Never

How did you find the questionnaire? Was it revealing, interesting or a bit of everything?

The questionnaire is designed to reveal the truth and this always has to be balanced against the benefit it has for you in terms of knowledge. For you now know what is draining you of your energy and what you need to concentrate on improving. What patterns of behaviour do you need to stop and put right?

The importance of the answers to the questions, is not so much how many Frequentlys you have overall but what you discovered about yourself and your energy supply. Hence, there is no scoring system for the questionnaire. It is intended merely to highlight patterns of behaviour that you may not have been consciously aware of. For instance, you may have always felt to date that you were *self-critical*, but the questionnaire may have revealed that, in actual fact, the biggest drain on your energy, at this present moment, is *resentment*.

Taking action

The only thing that will stop your energy draining is taking positive action. The recommended action is to work through the 30-day programme outlined below. The programme allows you to work on an issue from the questionnaire every day for a minimum of four weeks. The focus is on your long-term pleasure.

Working with negative habits

To increase your energy supply you need to take positive and concerted action. For example, let's say *resentment* is the biggest drain on your energy. The cycle to date may have been, 'It's not fair', 'I am not that lucky', and 'I have less'. When working on an issue it is important to notice just how many resentful thoughts crop up during the day; then instead of going down your usual route of 'Unlucky me', 'Not for me', 'Unhappy me', replace these thoughts with positive thoughts such as 'Time for me', 'My turn' and 'Goody, me next' and notice the reaction both internally and externally.

The biggest thing to remember when working with your negative habits – whether it is anger, criticism or resentment – is that the process of change is always the same; it just needs to be worked through. The reason for the programme is that although most people are really good about doing things on Day 1, Day 2 or Day 3, they are not so good about doing it for a month, two months or three months. So why is that? The main reason is that people get excited about what is happening when they notice the initial results, and they want more of it, but they don't want to have to wait, so they give up doing the work. Your imagination is brilliant at running things forward. It allows you to think things like, 'Just imagine how wonderful I'll be and how much better I'll feel if I carry on with this' and then because your imagination allows you to believe that you have already arrived, your efforts and intentions to get there disappear. You give up before you start and you resist having to go through all the effort, even though you are certain that the results will be even more amazing than you could ever have believed.

The trick is to remain focused, however ridiculous, silly or even trivial it might appear at the time, and listen more to what's happening inside of you rather than running your imagination forward. For you will get there and it is worth doing all the clearing work because when you do arrive you'll be fresher, lighter, freer, calmer and more relaxed as a person.

Remember, if you are committed and you really work on something you are bound to go through phases when you think you are not making progress and perhaps even more resentful, angry or critical thoughts will crop up. This is normal because as soon as you deal with one issue another issue will crop up, seemingly to try to spoil your efforts. Stick to the programme in this book for as long as you can, because there is a lot to discover and there may be a fair amount of clearing work to do. Possibly there may be days when you don't want to be bothered but stick at it. The programme is for 30 days, just one month's work. Good luck and give it a try. The benefits are there for you.

Creating more energy

You need to create and restock your energy regularly. By getting in touch with your beliefs and opinions you now know what is preventing you from having access to this infinite supply of energy. The questionnaire clearly identified which negative beliefs or issues are preventing you from maintaining your energy supply. In future, instead of relying upon control, criticism, anger, compromise, revenge, regret, resentment, worry and judgment, which are depleting your energy day-in and day-out in your job, you can choose different thoughts and become more energetic and energised at work. You have to feel energised in order to be energising and to feel energised you have first to deal with your conscious and unconscious 'resistance' to being energetic.

To access the energy in you, you have to go beyond your 'mind' and focus on your 'heart', wherein lie the feelings that put you in touch with everything you need to know. Within your mind, all of your beliefs, attitudes and survival games are stored. You can create all sorts of blocks to keep you from experiencing that great energy. Your mind is a real dustbin, if you like, that clogs up your energy flow. However, these issues have served a purpose in keeping you in a static position until you 'got it' or learnt the necessary lesson. The lesson may have been very painful, a bit tricky or difficult to appreciate but it usually was something that you needed to experience.

Building your energy

The 30-day programme encourages you to be open and enthusiastic while you learn and experience more about your new thoughts and beliefs. It is not just about whether your feelings are positive or negative. You need to treat each thought with equal enthusiasm and openness.

Let's look at the programme in more detail. The programme

asks you to look at all your energy drainers in turn for 15 minutes each day for ten days. You then repeat the process a second and a third time in order to really deal with each negative habit fully. You will spend five minutes feeling and recalling all of your resistance to the subject; then you will spend five minutes feeling all of your desire for the positive trait and then five minutes feeling grateful for all the times when you have experienced that positive trait.

Most people do the programme first thing in the morning but it works equally well at lunchtime or just before you go to bed. It is important to stick to the programme and to complete it at the same time every day, if you can.

Days 1, 11 and 21

Experience the feelings, thoughts and emotions that stop you being *calm*.

Sit in a chair or lie down and prepare yourself for your 15-minute personal development session.

For five minutes, feel all of your *resistance* to being and acting calmly in your job. Experience all of your negative thoughts and your angry feelings such as, 'I don't like being left out', 'I am angry about the way she spoke to me', or 'I don't like being taken advantage of.'

Now for a further five minutes feel your intense *desire* to be calm at work and imagine how wonderful your job could be if you were really, really calm.

Finally, for the last five minutes *feel grateful* for all the times when you were calm, cool or detached at work.

When you have finished, you may want to write down what came up for you. Now take this calm feeling with you into work today and notice how differently you respond.

Days 2, 12 and 22

Experience the feelings, thoughts and emotions that stop you being *open-minded*.

Sit in a chair or lie down and prepare yourself for your 15-minute personal development session.

For five minutes, feel all of your *resistance* to being open-minded in your job. Experience all of your negative thoughts and your critical comments such as, 'I really should be able to do this quicker', 'Haven't you finished that yet?', or 'I think your work is just sloppy and careless.'

Now for five minutes feel your intense *desire* to be open-minded and how much simpler and easier your job would be and how much more people would trust and open up to you.

Finally, for the last five minutes *feel grateful* for all the times when you remained open-minded at work. Remember how easy it was and how grateful people were for your kindness and acceptance of them.

When you have finished, you may want to scribble down any notes or points of interest. Now take this open-minded attitude with you into work and notice how willing people are to share things with you.

Days 3, 13 and 23

Experience the feelings, thoughts and emotions that stop you being *assertive*.

Sit in a chair or lie down and prepare yourself for your 15-minute personal development session.

For five minutes, feel all of your *resistance* to being assertive in your job. Experience all of your negative thoughts and any compromising attitudes you may have, such as your feelings of inadequacy, fear or uncertainty to speak up for yourself and to tell people how you really feel. Recall all of the ways you swallow your words or hide your feelings.

Now for five minutes feel your intense *desire* to be assertive and imagine how much more powerful you would feel. Think about how relieved you'd feel at being able to stand up for yourself and be treated as you would like.

Finally, for the last five minutes *feel grateful* for all the times when you did achieve a certain level of assertiveness in your job. Remember how good it felt to stand up for what you felt and how easy it was to say 'No, thanks', or 'I'd prefer . . .', or 'I feel . . .'

When you have finished, write down anything that is important to you. Now, take this assertive feeling with you into work and notice just how easy it is to be honest and speak openly to people.

Days 4, 14 and 24

Experience the feelings, thoughts and emotions that stop you *giving*.

Sit in a chair or lie down and prepare yourself for your 15-minute personal development session.

For five minutes feel all of your *resistance* to giving to your job, your colleagues or to anyone in need. Experience all of your negative thoughts and feelings about giving such as, 'I'll get you back', 'I've done my giving', or 'It's my turn to receive now.'

Now for five minutes feel your intense *desire* to be able to give to others at work, whether it is in the form of time, support, money, information or knowledge. Feel how good it feels to give to others, even your so-called enemies, and notice how much lighter you feel.

Finally, for the last five minutes *feel grateful* for all the times when you have given willingly and taken the opportunity to give to others at work. Remember how wonderful it was to see their face, hear their voice or receive their thanks and how it made you feel worthwhile, of value or maybe needed.

When you have finished, make any notes and then take this giving feeling with you into work. Notice how you are willing to

give and respond to others and how people are willing to give
back to you.

Days 5, 15 and 25

**Experience the feelings, thoughts and emotions that stop you
accepting yourself and others.**

Sit in a chair or lie down and prepare yourself for your 15-minute
personal development session.

For five minutes, feel all of your *resistance* to being accepting in
your job. Experience all of your negative and judgmental thoughts
such as, 'I don't think he is worth promoting', 'He won't do as
good a job as me', or 'She isn't up to much.' Notice how you knock
yourself as well.

Now for five minutes feel your intense *desire* to be more
accepting towards yourself and others at work. Think about how
wonderful it would be to be accepted for who you are right now.
What would change? What dramas could you drop? How much
better would you feel about yourself?

Finally, for the last five minutes *feel grateful* for all the times
when you did accept others at work despite their mistakes,
criticisms or negative comments and did not feel the need to
retaliate or take offence. Notice how good you felt and how
relieved the other person was in return.

When you have finished, write down your findings and then
take this feeling of acceptance with you into work. Notice how
different it feels to accept others and to be accepted in return.

Days 6, 16 and 26

**Experience the feelings, thoughts and emotions that stop you
being *optimistic*.**

Sit in a chair or lie down and prepare yourself for your 15-minute
personal development session.

For five minutes, feel all of your *resistance* to being optimistic at work. Experience all of your negative thoughts and your regretful feelings such as, 'I wish I'd listened more and found out the exact reason, rather than jumping to my own conclusion', 'I wish I had made amends', or 'I wish I could have handled that situation better.'

Now for five minutes feel your intense *desire* to be optimistic at work and imagine how wonderful it would be if you could turn your thinking around. Think about all the possibilities and opportunities open to you in your job. How much lighter would you feel?

Finally, for the last five minutes *feel grateful* for all the times when you did manage to remain optimistic at work. Remember how doors that you had previously thought were closed suddenly opened up and how good it felt for you and everyone concerned.

When you have finished, write down your notes and then take this feeling of optimism into work today. Notice how positivity creates more positivity and how much easier it is to perform under these conditions.

Days 7, 17 and 27

Experience the feelings, thoughts and emotions that stop you being *content*.

Sit in a chair or lie down and prepare yourself for your 15-minute personal development session.

For five minutes, feel all of your *resistance* to being content in your job. Experience all of your negative thoughts and your feelings such as, 'It is not fair', ' I have less than others', or 'I feel my job takes too much out of me.'

Now for five minutes feel your intense *desire* to be content about the way it is. OK, it isn't perfect and you may prefer other things to be happening but get used to accepting how it is right here and right now. Realise that there is joy in accepting what you are and what you have in the present.

Finally, for the last five minutes *feel grateful* for all the times when you did just let it be. Remember how free, peaceful and content you felt.

When you have finished, you may want to write your findings down and then take this feeling of contentment with you into work and notice how much better you feel.

Days 8, 18 and 28

Experience the feelings, thoughts and emotions that stop you *trusting*.

Sit in a chair or lie down and prepare yourself for your 15-minute personal development session.

For five minutes, feel all of your *resistance* to trusting while you are at work. Experience all of your negative thoughts and feelings such as, 'What if it doesn't happen?' 'What if he doesn't do as he promised?' and 'What do I need to be doing?'

Now for five minutes feel your intense *desire* to really trust that everything is working out just fine and in your best interest. Notice how good it feels to trust that you are making the right decisions and choices at work.

Finally, for the last five minutes *feel grateful* for the things that have happened at work when you did let go and trust events, people or circumstances to run their course. Remember how much freer you felt and how much more time you had as a result.

When you have finished, you may want to write things down and then take this feeling of trust with you into work and notice how much lighter you feel.

Days 9, 19 and 29

Experience the feelings, thoughts and emotions that stop you being *relaxed*.

Sit in a chair or lie down and prepare yourself for your 15-minute personal development session.

For five minutes, feel all of your *resistance* to being relaxed in your job. Experience all of your negative thoughts and all of your worrying thoughts such as, 'I am worried about letting go', 'I am scared in case I make a wrong decision', or 'I am so fearful about my health, money situation or my future.'

Now for five minutes feel your intense *desire* to relax at work and let all the fear out. Feel the weight, the strain and the heaviness dropping off you.

Finally, for the last five minutes *feel grateful* for all the times when you did manage to be relaxed and react spontaneously and ultimately have a good time at work.

When you have finished, you may want to write things down and then go to work feeling relaxed and just notice how much easier it is to work when you are relaxed.

Days 10, 20 and 30

Experience the feelings, thoughts and emotions that stop you being *'more'* at work.

Sit in a chair or lie down and prepare yourself for your 15-minute personal development session.

For five minutes, feel all of your *resistance* to offering 'more' to your job. Experience all of your negative thoughts and feelings such as, 'I am afraid I wouldn't be able to offer more every day', 'I am scared in case others think I'm being silly', or 'I don't want to have to make the effort, as I like the way I am.'

Now for five minutes feel your intense *desire* to reach your full potential and to let go of all limiting thoughts. Feel yourself grow in confidence, self-esteem and power. Imagine that people are saying to you, 'I really appreciate your efforts and contribution', 'I am so grateful that you did what you did', 'Your effort and actions made a real difference', 'Your kindness lifted me so much', 'I knew you would achieve it', 'I always believed you had the potential to do something special', 'You deserve that award', 'Your job must have real meaning', 'You always have time for others', 'Thank you'.

Finally, for the last five minutes *feel grateful* for all the times when you did go that extra bit further than your job description, when you did put yourself out for the benefit of others. Remember how it helped you and the other person.

When you have finished, commit to offering more to the people who you come into contact with at work today. Remember they deserve to receive your contribution and you are in the position to offer it. Make someone's day special today and notice how special you feel as a result.

Summary of the programme

The biggest thing this programme creates is the realisation that it is so important to be caring at work. It is only by doing the programme consistently for 30 days that the real changes can be realised. For it allows you to recognise and see your own value and, in doing so, you begin that all-important process of allowing yourself to risk 'giving of yourself' within the job environment. It is only when you start to 'give' of yourself that you start to notice that almost everyone has an issue with giving. Paid salaried jobs can tempt you to become incredibly comfortable and complacent. Complacency means that you feel safe and secure. It also means, however, that you will put up with things because you don't want your security threatened in any way. For example, do you hate your job but love your salary? Would you quit your job if your salary was cut or stopped? Would you work for free? How much of yourself do you give for free?

If the issue is money rather than making a difference then the issue will always be one of money – 'my money'. However, if the issue is about making a difference then you have to give of yourself and allow yourself to be vulnerable. Sure, it may feel different, unusual or uncomfortable but if you want to make a difference you may have to do your job differently. The ten qualities within the programme are designed to help you do just that. They are there to lift you up to a higher and higher level of self-awareness and personal understanding, and can be used over and over again as you progress within your job and your career.

Step Four – Job Fulfilment

How passionate are you about your work? Is work the love of your life? How much of a people person are you? You will discover in the pages that follow that there is no set way or set thing that you have to do in order to achieve more job fulfilment. It is about consistently building your own level of personal job satisfaction.

Being passionate about your work and having good relationships with your work colleagues is essential if you want to achieve more in terms of job fulfilment. Passion isn't brash, flashy or external; it is an intensely personal thing. It is all about the 'inner you'. It is about discovering what drives you, what makes you tick and what make you feel truly alive, energised and of value. It involves only you, your skills, capabilities and qualities and how you can give more of yourself to the work world. Hence achieving spark within a job is often described as 'completing the jigsaw', finding the missing link or as 'finding the missing part of you'.

Your journey towards love or passion for your job has already begun because you have started, if you hadn't done so before, the process of speaking your truth, amending your reactions, highlighting areas for your self-development and building your energy supply. This part of the book is all about rediscovering you, your ideals, your lost dreams or hopes. It is about discovering that inner, passionate, innocent part of you, which realises that you have to do something constructive and positive about any niggling thoughts, feelings or wake-up calls. It is about achieving a sense of peace, balance and acceptance towards your job so that you can honestly say that your job is fulfilling, purposeful, motivating, rewarding and energising rather than forever worrying that you are wasting your time, potential and life. Achieving this state needs something from you in return, which is commitment in terms of time and effort. The result will be that you no longer ask yourself whether you are in the right job or fear being derailed or made redundant but you know that you are on track pursuing a new and purposeful challenge. You may even go as far as to know that you are leaving your individual and meaningful mark on the work world. The difference you decide to make may be large or small, national or international, personal or impersonal. The important point is that you are doing it today.

This is why finding and achieving job fulfilment is often described as 'the missing piece of the jigsaw' because people receive so much back in return. For some it is an increase in self-esteem and self-confidence. For others it is an inner knowing that they have made a difference to commerce, industry, the environment and/or other people's lives. And for others it is the fact that their work has turned into a purposeful mission and experience for them. Excited? Great! This is why job fulfilment holds such a high price because it cannot be bought or sold; it can only be experienced.

And sometimes it is the experience that can frustrate people because they know they want it but they can't quite get there quickly enough. Is this the case for you? Have you been knocking on new doors and wondering why they still remain closed? Have you perhaps not found the door? Or are you just restless and wish you could get on with the whole process quickly?

All of the above reactions are great and a really positive sign. A sign that you want to see the 'whole picture', 'vision' or 'mission' but you can't quite see it yet. The truth is you are not meant to.

When doors remain closed on your quest for job fulfilment, it is because you need to learn or grasp something about yourself, your situation or circumstances. It is a sign that you may need to do some more 'inner work'. So if this is the case try to resist the temptation to 'fix' it, and refer back to and work on those ten positive energy traits or your beliefs about work. This will help you shake yourself loose from your over-involvement in work and focus on the really important issue which is *you*.

The following chapters are all about your self-development because it is *you* who has to change, not the work world. It is about you recognising your talents and areas of pure excellence and tapping into them. Once you begin to define what you want and know yourself better you'll become unstoppable. Barriers once unrecognised suddenly become visible and once seen you can begin to remove, avoid or sidestep them. You have to be prepared to believe in yourself and to make plans to fulfil your perception of spark. You know what is important to you, even if you can't verbalise it yet, and what you can offer. The following chapters outline in quick, simple and easy steps what you need to focus on. Are you ready?

Let's step back in time for a moment and consider the career choices that led you to where you are today. What was good about them? Do you feel that some decisions were a mistake? The temptation will always be to look backwards rather than forwards – backwards at what might have been or backwards at what may have happened and at what you have put up with and allowed to happen.

So what has happened? Have you allowed yourself to cruise in your career for a bit too long? Have you allowed things to run their course and to shape themselves? Whatever has happened has happened for a reason and so regret is only going to take up more of your time, energy and ideas. There is no such thing as peddling backwards – even for those who change profession, field of work or job (see Case Study 5). For there is only the now and the present. There is some good news, though. All your skills, experience and knowledge to date are transferable, and the only thing that can run out is your desire. Your desire to step out of your comfort zone, your present circumstances and to *commit* to something that isn't wholly visible at present.

Your desire

Do you have a desire to do something special? The extent to which you realise this depends largely upon your upbringing, beliefs and experiences. Let's step back in time and do a quick 'passion check'. As a child you probably had more passion than you have today. Take a look at the list below and reflect on the past. What did you dream about becoming as a child? Tick or circle the one that is most relevant to you or add one of your own to the list.

• a doctor	• a veterinary	• a nurse
• a teacher	surgeon	• a fire fighter
• a police officer	• a writer	• a chef
• a baker	• a paramedic	• an actor
• a waitress	• a fisherman	• a waiter
• a photographer	• a reporter	• a diver
• a flight attendant	• a train driver	• a scientist
• an accountant	• a musician	• a pilot
• a farmer	• a lawyer	• a ballet dancer
• a librarian	• a stockbroker	• a rubbish collector
• an electrician	• a postman	• a mechanic
• a builder	• a designer	• a self-made
• a broadcaster	• a racing driver	millionaire
• a dentist	• a plumber	• a famous person

Children dream, fantasise and believe everything is possible for them. They think in terms of what they want, desire or would like to become. They research, role-play and even dress up in the clothes of their chosen profession. Children accept their innocence, naïvety and ignorance and enjoy their new-found freedom and expanse of possibilities. Children, above all, look to their elders or role models to endorse, support and help them create their job opportunities.

Once within a job and a company structure, the maturing person then usually looks to the company personnel department or manager to advise them about their future career progression and possible career paths. Up until now this has commonly been the chosen path in terms of careers and career advancement for many people. The emphasis has been on 'Mr Organisation' out there to help, advise and structure the individual's career path. Has that been true for you too? Do you look to your company or organisation to decide your career progression and career path? Do you look to the organisation and management to provide you with motivation, training and/or support?

In the past 20 years, business has changed drastically. Companies and organisations have become more globally focused. Increasingly the focus is on how to maintain a competitive advantage and improve the market position. High emphasis is placed on reducing overheads, meeting budgets and achieving higher profits. An individual's efficiency, targets and goals are higher than ever on the agenda. Organisations understandably want results and thus they expect results from their employees too. Market share, profits and share prices affect the way employees are now regarded by the company. There is less tolerance for poor, average or mediocre employees.

Results are now very much the 'order of the day' in terms of the modern business and economic world. An employee's career direction and career development is increasingly left to the employee to determine. As a result, personal desires can often get lost or forgotten in this intense atmosphere and pressure on improving overall performance. Did your desire get shelved in your attempt to do a good job or to be seen as a valuable member of the team? Have you, over time, forgotten about your desire?

Have the organisation's demands and pressures taken hold of you? Have you almost become conditioned to 'being' this company or organisation? Have you 'lost' yourself in the huge company structure? Do you know what you actually desire now? Maybe it was such a long time ago when you actually thought about yourself. Have you spent so many years being accountable to someone else's demands that you have become almost scared of or unused to thinking and deciding about your own career issues? Is this applicable to you?

The emphasis is now on 'you'; not your company, organisation or employer. The key, though, is to take a very positive view of everything that has happened to date. Remind yourself that everything has occurred for a reason and every experience adds to your understanding and perception of the business/work world. Don't be tempted to think negatively about the past but start to plan a brighter, purposeful future for yourself.

The whole concept behind the remaining chapters is to hand-hold you through the process that will unlock you from the organisation and redefine and establish your needs, desires and aspirations in terms of your job. It is a wonderful process of self-discovery and self-realisation, the bottom line of which is that you still have a very important and special contribution to make. The question is, 'Are you ready to define and fulfil this contribution?'

Defining job fulfilment

Work only becomes special, pleasurable and meaningful if it means something to you. Becoming fulfilled by your job is all about fine-tuning what you really think about your job or career. Thus, it is all about defining your emotions and feelings towards your job.

Being fulfilled is about continuously building it into your job on a day-to-day basis rather than having it today and not tomorrow. Job fulfilment is about increasing your knowledge of you and your job and about building up a whole host of experiences, which in turn builds your confidence and demonstrates that you are a valuable asset to your organisation. Too often people forget the building bit and get carried away by emotions and what seems like a good idea at the time. For example, people start off by being fulfilled by their job and are quite happy for a while; then they get used to it and they are less fulfilled by their job and start to make mistakes, offer less or perform less. The key to having fulfilment long-term is to define it for yourself and to keep it filled up – for fulfilment is what gives your career meaning, purpose and direction. If you are not fulfilled by your job you will come unstuck, reach a halt or start to drift off at a tangent. You need to define what job fulfilment means to you and then work on achieving it.

Choose and commit yourself to the things that will give you pleasure within your current job. All you have to do is pinpoint the things that will help you feel better about your work and then if you work at putting them in place, you will start to feel more energised, creative and of value. Work only feels awkward, difficult or out of balance when you have more of what you don't want and less of what you *do* want. If this is how it is for you, or if you are unable to define what you want in terms of fulfilment, complete the following exercise. From the list of words below, circle about five things that you really want more of from your job.

Exercise

In my job I need more:

• Fun	• Recognition	• Money
• Creativity	• Respect	• Friends
• Flexibility	• Calmness	• Compassion
• Kindness	• Opportunity	• Company
• Challenge	• Laughter	• Honesty
• Skill	• Attention	• Vision
• Common Sense	• Training	• Buzz

- Power
- Tolerance
- Purpose
- Capacity to accept
- Say
- Patience
- Compliance
- Feeling of leaving a legacy
- Visibility
- Ability
- Value

Now, go back over your choice of words and take another look. This isn't a 'wish' list; it is a contract that you are going to make with yourself. For these are the things that you feel would give your job or career that necessary fulfilment, but bear in mind you may need to reassess things in six months' time. Your highlighted words are some of the missing ingredients and just as very little yeast is needed to make the dough rise, you will need a small amount of these things in order to make a *huge* difference to the way you feel about your job.

Once you have defined what you want more of from your current job, visualise yourself actually having it. What does it look like? What does it feel like? What action have you taken? Having a vision means being active rather than passive and constantly reviewing your fulfilment levels. The best way to achieve the things you have highlighted on the above list is to use people to help you. Watch, talk to and draw upon the people around you who possess the qualities that you are searching for. These people could be working alongside, above or below you but what is important is that they can help you. Whether or not they are willing to help you depends heavily upon your ability to communicate. Good communication involves your ability to use rapport, pace and the appropriate style. So let's just cover the essential facts so that you can gain the most from your working relationships.

Communication

Communication is crucial to achieving good working relationships. How you choose to communicate with your work colleagues can seriously affect your job and ultimately your career progression. When the communication between you and your colleagues is good, the relationships feel relaxed, open and honest; but when the communication between you and your colleagues is poor, the relationships can feel cold, strained, tense and as if one person is withholding from another in some way.

The purpose of this section is to show you how to improve the communication between you and your colleagues so that ultimately you can achieve what you are looking for from the relationships and hence the job.

About communication

Do you feel from time to time that you are unable to communicate with certain people at work, or that you can't do the right thing, or that you are always being misunderstood? The answer to improving your work relationships lies in improving your communication style. Your communication style determines whether you:

• Get on with your work colleagues
• Can accept each other's differences and similarities
• Understand each other
• Have open and honest conversations
• And can work through things to achieve a positive outcome.

Initially as the one who is looking for job fulfilment it is up to you to instigate and carry out any change to your communication style. (In time, as your work colleagues change their attitude and behaviour towards you, you'll feel that your efforts and changes were worthwhile.) You are going to need to hold the positive vision – a vision of building better communication skills between you and your work colleagues. Hence focus on the long-term pleasure rather than the short-term pain.

What is good communication?

Good communication is about you being aware of your communication style and your colleagues' preferred communication styles, and being flexible in your dealings with your colleagues. Good communication is about achieving:

- A balance of speaking and sharing
- Good listening skills
- A grasp of the situation and facts before you speak.

Developing harmony

Harmonious relationships are relationships without barriers. Barriers can be created between yourself and your colleagues because somebody didn't do what was expected of them, say the right thing or get what they wanted. The most common barriers used are:

- Making excuses, complaining or moaning ('Unlucky me', page 46)
- Ignoring, avoiding or leaving the person out ('Cold' behaviour, page 47)
- Trying to talk over or show off to the other person ('I'm the best' behaviour, page 47).

Have you ever used any of the above barriers? Did they give you what you wanted? Have you ever felt, 'Why did I do that? If only I'd done something else instead'? The truth is, barriers rarely move relationships forward positively, so try to avoid using them.

Increasing communication awareness

Are you aware that only a small percentage of the impression you make on your work colleagues stems from verbal communication? The words you use only make up around 5 per cent of what you 'say'. Your non-verbal messages have a far greater impact on your colleagues. In fact, some research goes as far as to say that 80 per cent of what you 'say' is non-verbal. The remaining 15 per cent is through the 'way' you say things. To clarify, non-verbal communication includes the following:

- Voice pitch and emphasis
- Pace
- Breathing
- Posture/stance
- Facial expression
- Eye contact
- Eye movements
- Pupil size
- Standing positions
- Gestures/movements
- Dress style
- Status symbols.

Body language

Body language has often been described as the *real* language. How good are you at picking up the body's signals? Do you instinctively know whether your work colleagues like or dislike you?

The important thing with regard to body language is to give clear signals. For example, say what you mean and communicate this in your body language; otherwise confusion arises and then lack of trust can develop between you and your colleagues.

Communication is all about the truth. Can you handle the truth and do you respect those who do speak the truth? *The message is*: tell your colleagues what you are feeling because even if you don't, your facial expressions will!

The eyes

Your pupil size affects the way your message is received. It is now believed that as well as pupils being affected by light, there is a direct link between the size of the pupil and the interest of the subject. For example, the greater your interest in any subject the bigger your pupils and the less often you blink. Are you making your subject interesting enough?

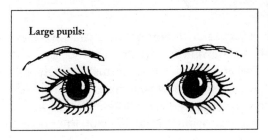

Large pupils may signify:
- Excitement
- Truthfulness
- Directness
- Openness
- Relaxed.

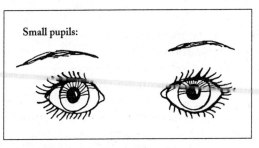

Small pupils may signify:
- Loss of spark
- Uncertainty
- Unhappiness
- Anger
- Fear
- Tiredness
- Sadness.

The position of the shoulders

People tend to raise their shoulders when tense and lower them when relaxed. When you wish to talk to your colleagues about something important, gauge your colleague's receptiveness by checking the general positioning of their shoulders and head. Raised shoulders, a lowered head and a drooping mouth indicate a tense, negative or non-receptive person.

The position of the head

- **A raised head** may signify openness, excitement, positivity and power over the situation.
- **A lowered head** can indicate doubt, fear, anger, dissatisfaction, loss of interest and uncertainty.
- **A tilted sideways head** may mean interest, curiosity or possibly coyness.

Clear signals

With any communication it is important that you give clear signals. Clear signals are transmitted when your thoughts and words tally. When this happens your body forms a straight line from head to foot. Thus, being aware of your posture will help you communicate a clearer message to your colleagues. How do you stand at present? Do you lean against a wall for support or do you stand tall?

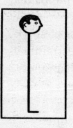

Standing in an upright position demonstrates a person who is comfortable with the situation as their thoughts and actions are in agreement and complement each other. There are no 'hidden' agendas in the communication.

Leaning forward demonstrates a person who wants to discipline, influence or control another, and is normally an indication of someone adopting a 'Questioner' or 'I'm the best' behaviour (page 47).

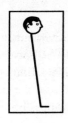

Leaning back indicates a person who is defensive or slightly unsure of themselves in the situation, and is normally associated with someone adopting a 'Unlucky me' or 'Cold' behaviour (pages 46–7).

All the above postures show a clear correlation between thoughts and words. What is your posture like? Do you need to amend anything?

Rapport

Building good communication skills is also about developing 'rapport'. Rapport is the basis for harmony in any conversation. When you have rapport things often feel so good that it is easy to lose sight of the time. Do you enjoy rapport? Do you sometimes have trouble recreating rapport in subsequent conversations? Do you know why?

When rapport exists between you and your colleagues it is a silent knowing but one that is also obvious to the people around you. Rapport is the basis of a working relationship, which is why it is so central to your communication style. Rapport exists between you and your colleagues when you and your colleagues can demonstrate a sense of *oneness*. When rapport exists there is a mutual feeling of harmony, wellbeing and, of course, respect for each other.

To begin to create positive rapport in your relationships, it is necessary to focus on the similarities between you and your colleagues. For example, focus on the things you agree on, feel and think the same about. By concentrating on the similarities it will help you to build good relationships and overcome and dissolve any resistance, distrust, fear or doubt. If you have rapport, you can nearly always solve any differences, but if rapport is absent the focus is nearly always on your differences.

Pacing

The best tool for achieving rapport is pace and if you can master it you can create harmony in all your relationships at work. Pace is all about showing that you:

- Agree with the person
- See where the person is coming from
- Understand the person
- Share similar likes, dislikes and beliefs
- Appreciate the person's point of view.

Pace occurs naturally between people who get on. To achieve pace at work you need to be able to mirror the other person's body language, voice, vocabulary and mood in such a way that this person feels comfortable and at ease with you. In short, pace validates the person's feelings and thoughts and opens up the channel of communication between you.

Methods of pacing
- **Body language** – sitting position, hand and arm movements, overall posture, angle of the head, dress style, facial expressions and standing position.
- **Speech** – pitch, pace, tone, volume, inflection, vocabulary, business jargon, buzz words and technical terms.
- **Mood** – attitude, vision, belief, enthusiasm, tolerance, involvement, respect for your colleagues' skills, qualities and knowledge.

Pacing avoids conflict
You know what it is like to catch the attention of someone in the office or in the corridor and the other person uses an air of 'busyness' in order to ignore you. How does displacing of this sort make you feel? Irritated, annoyed or maybe angry? Think how different you would have felt if the other person had given you eye contact, a friendly nod or a sign that says, 'I've seen you. Just give me a moment to finish this and I'll pop over to

talk to you.' Yes, it is that simple, but it makes a big difference to your mood, the way you view that person and feel about yourself.

Improve your relationships with your work colleagues by pacing your conversations with them.

Example of pacing

Have you ever promised someone something and then only remembered your promise when the person reminded you? How well did you pace the other person? Or did you show the person your irritation?

Example: As soon as you arrive at work your colleague calls out to you saying, 'Great you are in early today, as you promised that you'd show me to do those whizzy new things on the computer.' You answer with a note of irritation in your voice, without looking at your colleague, 'Oh dear, did I really? All right, if I promised, set up your computer and we'll do it now.' Your body language says, 'The sooner we get started the sooner we'll be finished.'

There is nothing wrong with the above but the rapport is lost. To create rapport and pace it might have worked better if you had replied by looking at your colleague and maintaining their enthusiasm by saying, 'Thank goodness you reminded me. I had forgotten all about our agreement. Well, I really want to show you how to do that but I need five to 10 minutes to get my head round it, so you get the computer set up and I'll be there as soon as I'm ready.'

The latter response will have a much more positive outcome and it is all due to *pace*. If you can match the colleague's enthusiasm and energy but also give yourself the necessary time to get into the right frame of mind, the outcome will be more successful.

Choose a couple of situations where you feel you have displaced your colleagues and let's work on them. Recall how you displaced someone at work. Was it your voice, your look, posture or facial expressions? Write down how you would do it differently next time.

Exercise
I displaced my work colleague by:

In the above example – expressing my frustration by looking away and pretending not to be interested. I showed my colleague that I had very little time and that I wanted to be quick and get the task over and done with.

Next time I would be different because I would:

In the above example – I would be more honest and share my feelings with my colleague. I would explain that I had forgotten and that I wanted to keep my promise. I would explain that I was pushed for time at the moment and I would agree a time when we were to complete the task together. I would match my colleague's enthusiasm.

Try repeating the exercise several times with other examples of when you felt you displaced your colleagues and consider how you would choose to be different next time.

Verbal communication

Verbal communication is a big subject. As previously stated it makes up roughly 15 per cent of your overall message (body language is 85 per cent) but your choice of words and the way they are delivered can make your working relationships easy or difficult.

Awareness

As with everything else, if you really want to resolve a verbal issue then become aware of the following:

- Decide who owns the problem
- Clarify what your needs are
- Choose a more effective verbal style.

Who owns the problem?

As was mentioned in Step Two, if you want a situation to change then you have to own the problem and set about resolving the issue between you and your work colleague. Remember it is easy to take the credit when things are running smoothly in the office but it is much tougher to own the problem in the face of difficulties. On those days, it would be much simpler and easier if you could blame your boss or your colleagues. And the most common way to do this would be through your language. For example, to criticise, to embarrass, to tell off or to pick at. But verbal attacks don't work in the long run and they only create more of the same. 'Owning' the problem means that the cycle of 'blame' gets broken and that it is much easier to focus on your needs and ultimately the solution itself.

Needs?

What you say and what the other person chooses to hear can be two different things. How your colleagues receive your message is often the bit that gets overlooked. It is, however, a very important part of the communication style because it affects the way your colleague feels, responds or views you. You always have a choice, which is either: Do I deal with this positively or do I deal with this negatively? A negative response would be to:

- Ignore the reaction
- Brush it off
- Argue that your colleague was in the wrong because either they overreacted, didn't hear what was said, misinterpreted it or didn't understand the situation.

Negative responses only create blocks that blame the other person and thereby teach others to build up resentments towards you. Your colleagues need to receive a positive response when they express how they heard your message. A positive response would be:

- Listening to your colleague
- Allowing your colleague to say what they actually heard
- Allowing your colleague to express their feelings
- Acknowledging where the misunderstanding occurred
- Validating their feelings
- Asking them what would help them
- Discussing the way forward together.

The spoken word

The spoken word is sometimes open to interpretation. Nobody likes to be misquoted but then equally nobody likes to be told that they have made something up or overreacted.

Do you plod along, not really giving much thought to the words you actually speak? Are you aware of the spoken word only when something goes wrong; for example, if you:

- Don't get what you want from a conversation
- Don't get the reaction you expected from your colleague
- Or someone says something that hurts you or presses one of your buttons.

When this occurs, are you forced to take a closer look at what is actually coming out of your mouth? If you went out to purchase a new computer, a photocopier, or a mobile phone, you would probably check that the instructions were safely in the box before you bought it. But how much do you know about your mind? Have you read up on the subject or are you perhaps:

- Scared of it?
- Unsure of what you'll discover?
- Or believe it is only for the experts?

But is it? In the last decade a lot has been discovered and written about how you can improve your relationships, especially those with your work colleagues. Have you ever said something you didn't mean, wish you hadn't said or regretted afterwards? Of course you have! What's important to note is when there is a misunderstanding. Misunderstandings occur most when you or your colleagues are:

- Busy
- Tired
- Ill
- Emotional
- Distracted
- In a new environment
- Under pressure
- Or inexperienced.

These and many other situations occur not because of a failure of your mind but as a result of using your mind in a negative way, often unintentionally. However, now is the time to use your mind in more positive and fulfilling ways.

How your mind works

If you understand how your mind works then you can use it positively to:

- Communicate better with your colleagues
- Avoid stressful or unpleasant scenarios
- Make better decisions
- Gain an overall view of the situation
- Be more relaxed
- Avoid doing what you've always done
- Achieve your goals and objectives
- Solve issues with others more quickly
- Enjoy yourself more.

Your mind records information, facts, feelings, emotions, sounds, smells and voices in the same way as a CD holds information. Press the right button in your mind and you can be transported back in time to almost any event:

- Your first promotion
- Your favourite boss
- Your first day at work
- Your flirtatious moments in the office
- Your biggest pay cheque.

It is thought that all your experiences throughout life are recorded in your mind and can be played back at any time in response to the right stimulus. This is good news when your favourite love song comes on the radio as it can be a marvellous reminder of that romantic hot holiday. However, when someone cuts you down in a meeting, the mind can play the fury, irritation and frustration of previous similar occasions; hence your possible negative reaction and/or response.

Sigmund Freud developed the theory that each person is made up of several different egos and in the development of this theory, called Transactional Analysis, the mind is thought of as a combination of three tapes. These are:

1 **Parent tape** containing recordings of control as well as support and nurture.
2 **Adult tape** containing recordings of fact and common sense.
3 **Child tape** containing recordings of feelings – happy or upsetting ones.

All three mind types are equally good, have strong and weak points and can be appropriate under different circumstances. They are, however, unlikely to be of equal size, and the choice of tape determines how you respond or behave in certain situations at work.

The parent *mind tape*

The information recorded on this tape comes from your early experiences with your own parents and teachers. Remarks like 'Sit up straight', 'Get on with your work and do it accurately', 'Let me help you' are imprinted on your *parent* mind tape and can be played back. You can often hear the parent attitude at work in phrases such as: 'It's our policy to . . .' or 'It is best to do it this way.' The *parent* mind tape has two parts, namely the controlling and disciplining side and the supportive and caring side.

A person using their *controlling parent* mind tape would be more likely to be cross, angry and critical when a work colleague makes a mistake. Typical words used would include:

• Right and wrong
• Good and bad
• Never and always
• Sensible and careless.

A person using their *caring parent* mind tape, on the other hand, would be more likely to be understanding and sympathetic towards their colleague. Typical phrases used would include:

- I understand
- Never mind!
- As long as you are now aware
- Let me help you
- Do you need more time?

The adult *mind tape*

All facts, logical experiences and common sense are logged on the *adult* mind tape. This is the mature, understanding and sensible part of your personality. When you use this tape your words and gestures are logical and well-thought-out, as opposed to the more automatic reactions on the *parent* mind tape.

People use their *adult* mind tape at work when they collect information, evaluate it, work out possible solutions and seek to resolve things in a logical and calm way.

A person using their *adult* mind tape would ask open and specific questions in their interactions with their colleagues – questions such as:

- Who was involved?
- What is your reaction to . . . ?
- Where did it happen?
- What are your possible choices?
- How can this be resolved in the best possible way?

The child *mind tape*

The *child* mind tape represents the child you once were. On it are all your emotions – resolved or unresolved – your early experiences, together with your initial attitude to yourself and others. The *child* tape responds to situations instinctively and emotionally. Examples of a person using the *child* mind tape at work include phrases such as:

- I must
- It is mine
- Don't do that
- It's not my fault
- You idiot.

Your mind tapes

When you are under any kind of pressure at work you will revert to the tape most often used in a similar situation. The reaction is often spontaneous and you frequently don't have the time to assess whether it is the best and most suitable work response. It just happens.

So, let us discover which mind tape you are using the most at work – is it the *child*, *parent* or *adult* mind tape? Discover which one it is by completing the following examples.

Example 1: You are writing a report. The office is busy and noisy, and you are in a rush. All the equipment is in use and you need to photocopy something urgently. You suddenly spot that no one is using the photocopier nearest you; you approach it and suddenly another colleague pushes in front of you. What would your instinctive reaction be to this person? Think about your body language and words. Briefly describe your most likely response, then circle the mind tape that best describes your reaction.

My response:

Parent   **Adult**   **Child**

Example 2: You arrive at work exhausted after a two-hour delay to your journey. On your arrival you are told that you are late for a departmental meeting. You enter the room and everyone looks at you, horrified that you are late. What is your most likely reaction towards the people in the meeting? Briefly describe your likely response, then circle the mind tape that best describes your reaction.

My response:

Parent   Adult   Child

Example 3: Your computer has been used while you have been out of the office and accidentally broken by another colleague that you don't think much of. How would you be inclined to react when you found out? Briefly describe your likely response, then circle the mind tape that best describes your reaction.

My response:

Parent   Adult   Child

Example 4: After a long day at work, someone slips in front of you on your approach to a busy roundabout. In order to avoid crashing into them you have to brake hard. What is your instant reaction? Briefly describe it, then circle the mind tape that best describes your reaction.

My response:

Parent   **Adult**   **Child**

Example 5: Your boss bluntly points out that you made a mistake with some arrangements ridiculing you in front of all the other team members. How do you feel? How do you behave? Briefly describe it, then circle the mind tape that best describes your reaction.

My response:

Parent   **Adult**   **Child**

What is your dominant work tape?

Given that this is a limited questionnaire, was your dominant mind tape what you expected it to be? Gaining an insight into yourself helps to increase your ability to improve your interactions with your colleagues. Each mind tape, as you have seen, has its strong and weak points and, of course, in certain situations some tapes are better than others. For example: it is easier to come up with creative, innovative ideas when your *child* mind tape is switched on; it is easier to discuss and resolve a conflict with your colleagues when using your *adult* mind tape; and it is easier to comfort and reassure your colleagues when using your *caring parent* mind tape.

Unfortunately that is not always the case – people often reprimand their staff by using their *child* mind tape; try to create a fun, corporate entertainment day using their *adult* mind tape; or choose to discuss new ideas and concepts while using the *parent* mind tape.

Choosing which mind tape to play

It will help if you play the most suitable tape in any given work situation. Sometimes you will need to adopt the *parent* mind tape when you focus on the rules and regulations. At other times you will need the *caring parent* tape to support and help your colleagues, or you will need the *child* mind tape to come up with creative ideas and the *adult* tape to create open, honest business relationships. Listed below are a few helpful reminders:

1 **Be flexible and honest in your approach.** Change your tape if your strategy isn't working.
2 **Play the best tape for each work situation.** Assess your behaviour afterwards by thinking about what tape you used. Did your tape produce a good result? If it didn't, try adjusting the tape next time around. Does changing the tape make a difference?
3 **Be aware of your dominant tape** and its possible disadvantages. For instance:

- **A large *controlling parent* mind tape** creates a tendency for an individual to tell others what to do and does not listen to and encourage these colleagues to develop their own ideas.
- **A large *caring parent* mind tape** means that the individual will look after and mother their colleagues who don't see the need to develop their own level of self-reliance.
- **A large *adult* mind tape** – means that the individual can become reliant upon being regarded as having good opinions and views, so the individual may have difficulty letting go and having fun at work.

- A large *child* mind tape – creates a tendency for an individual to avoid setting themself goals and targets and ultimately taking responsibility for their actions.

4 **Avoid confusing tapes** when dealing with your colleagues, as it could lead to conflict. For example, if one person communicates a message and the other person chooses to play a different tape, which conveys a totally different message, conflict can arise:

- Colleague: 'Have you seen my report?' *Adult mind tape*
- You: 'Do I always have to remind you of everything?' *Child mind tape*

Developing your adult mind tape

The *adult* mind tape is highly effective and powerful in the business world. It forces individuals to take responsibility for themself and to build good working relationships. To develop your adult tape, you need to practise the following strategies:

- **Ask your business colleagues open questions** including, 'What would help you?', 'How can we resolve this?', 'What would be another way of looking at that?', 'What are you expected to do?'
- **Ask specific questions** including: 'Who is responsible?', 'How did it happen?', 'What would you like to do?'
- **Listen attentively**, use your body language to show you are listening, show empathy by your posture and expression and most of all allow your colleagues the time to express themselves.
- **Admit your mistakes**. A true adult admits when they make a mistake. So, if you have made a mistake or if you could have handled the situation better, admit it.
- **Check the facts**. Remain open-minded by checking out the facts within any given situation. Ask questions such as, 'Can you trust the source of that information?', 'Where did you hear that?', or 'Is this what you believe?'
- **Combine the *caring parent* mind tape with the *adult* mind tape** by saying things like, 'Yes, it is upsetting when you don't get

promoted, so what do you need to do to improve your performance?', 'It is natural to be disappointed but the feelings will
pass.'

There is a lot to take in here and as you try these new techniques
notice how small changes can bring about improvements in your
working relationships.

To sum up, you need excellent communications skills if you are
going to enlist your work colleagues to help you develop your
personal qualities (pages 102–3). The above techniques will
help you to create happy, successful and communicative working
relationships. Now, you need to identify from the list below how
the person can help you.

- **As a role model** – having a role model is an easy and worthwhile
  way in which to develop your own qualities. Watch your chosen
  person closely to see how they deal with different people, situations and problems. The role model can pass on tips and offer
  you advice and in doing so save you time, energy and effort in
  the long run. Remember the emphasis on the relationship is on
  learning and progression, and it is not about stealing energy
  from this person. The role model can be your boss or anyone
  who you feel has the *qualities you are looking for*.
- **As a mentor** – this relationship is different from having a role
  model because the mentor is not usually your boss but someone
  in the organisation that you can talk to. Someone who you
  don't necessarily come in contact with during your normal
  daily workings. The mentor will also benefit because they are
  building up a reputation for developing people within the
  organisation. The benefit to you is that the person can offer
  you open but confidential advice. The role of the mentor is to
  advise, encourage and talk from personal experience about you
  and your progress.
- **By networking with people who are fulfilled by their job** –
  networking can help keep you fulfilled. Meeting new people
  and keeping up-to-date can help you to stay fresh and upbeat.

Once that you have identified how the person can help you, see if you can create the relationship that you desire. The key to a successful working relationship is to have no attachment to it. That means that the focus of your energy is on the 'quality' that you are developing rather than the relationship itself. For there is no guarantee that the relationship will last or stay the same and there is every likelihood that when you have become what you aspired to be, the relationship will no longer hold the same attraction for you. Hence it may be necessary to 'let go' of the relationship once you have achieved what you set out to achieve, in order to create the room for new qualities to be identified and new relationships to develop and flourish as a result. You never stand still and need to constantly define qualities that you wish to develop. Create as many opportunities as you can to work alongside people who already have the qualities that you need to develop.

Step Five – Create a Real Purpose to Your Work

Having a real purpose is a crucial ingredient to becoming passionate about your job or work. Purpose is sometimes described as a work mission or, as I like to describe it, 'healing the space'. From now on, the term 'healing the space' will be used, as it can help you really to go beyond your commonly held concepts, beliefs or attitudes about your 'purpose'. However, if the term grates with you then simply choose something else more suitable, perhaps your mission, your contribution or alternatively your purpose.

'Healing the space' is, as the name implies, about giving something truly amazing, meaningful and, if you like, something everlasting. Why? Because it encourages you to go beyond the norm and it can represent something incredibly special to you, the one doing the 'giving', and also to the person receiving.

If you are the giver, you have the opportunity to feel of value, of worth and special because you are in the fortunate position to give or to make a significant difference. The receiver has the opportunity to feel special too because they are in the fortunate position of being in the company of someone who knows how to and is willing to give.

Giving is something that many people shy away from, avoid or perhaps even pretend they don't see the need to do anything about. 'Healing the space' is all about doing more, offering more and going beyond the set guidelines of many job descriptions. It is all to do with getting in tune with your power, your beliefs and your energy source. Your energy source is no longer tainted or spoilt by your own or other people's opinions, views or attitudes. It is also an energy source that is both powerful and gentle, for it has the capacity, drive and force to remove barriers, obstacles and threats, at the same time allowing you to be empathetic, understanding and considerate.

By putting your energy to good use, you can find ways to do what is right and just and more importantly do things that benefit others. You can use your energy not to make a quick monetary, business or personal gain but to make a difference to the lives of as many people as you can. Many people find that their attitude towards work changes from: 'I have . . .'

- A crummy job working for a small organisation
- A crummy job working for a big organisation
- A boring nine-to five job
- A dead-end job
- A high-flying, meaningless job
- A job, which pays the bills but which provides little or no personal satisfaction
- A job, which is good while it lasts!
- A job that kills my spirit
- Or a job that sucks everything out of me

to: 'I have a job that helps me to make a meaningful and important contribution to the world I live in.'

You may feel like running away and shouting, 'But am I ready, capable and equipped to do this?' The answer is, 'Yes, you are.' All you have to do is be willing to fulfil your new purpose in your present job or, if necessary, in a different job.

The big opportunity

'Healing the space' is about opening your eyes, being aware of your surroundings and responding to the needs of others within your current job situation or environment. 'Healing the space' does not necessarily mean a turnaround or a shift in direction. If it does, though, rest assured that your experience and skills to date will always be applicable or transferable.

When you have a mission to heal the space, you will truly have made a huge advance in your search for passion about your job. Having a desire to heal the space means that you have turned a corner. You will be able to see yourself for who you are and can stop trying 'to fit yourself to the job'. There is no point trying to fit in or be something you are not, just to suit others. You have your own unique and valuable contribution to make to the work world. Stop trying to be 'all things to all people'; spreading yourself thin is tiring and can be frustrating, so develop the desire that you need to heal the space.

Creating and developing a reason to make a difference is all about fine-tuning what you do in your job. It is all about defining your emotions and feelings towards your job. Your work really becomes exciting and something you are passionate about only if it means something to you. The concept of 'healing the space' encompasses your strongest beliefs, ambitions and vision for yourself.

Formulating your purpose is the next step. This involves making strong, powerful and dramatic statements about what you could do and be. The reason for doing this is that it is necessary to believe that your input helps you to get used to and to feel comfortable about taking responsibility for your own beliefs, ideas and energy supply. Encourage yourself to make your statements as powerful and as full of conviction as you can. Your statements then represent your new goals. You probably won't be able to achieve them instantly, as they usually represent your goals for the next five, ten or maybe 15 years, but you will need to fine-tune them regularly.

Get thinking and really try to get as passionate as you can about your thoughts and ideas. Passionate ideas create in themselves energy and enthusiasm, which in turn creates a huge, positive response in others. The expected responses will add more fuel, support and energy to your mission. Try to get really fired up and think about the things that really stir up your emotions. Emotions such as:

- That is not right!
- That is not fair!
- That is not just!
- That is appalling!
- That is not in accordance with human rights!
- That shouldn't exist in this day and age!
- That should be stopped!
- And finally, that needs my attention!

Give it your full attention and carry on giving it your full attention, even if some people around you look, stare, criticise or even laugh at you. For example, someone may say, 'So you think you are Superman/Superwoman now?' Such comments, which perhaps might once have stirred you and made you stop, retaliate or question your actions, now will merely convince you that you are on track, going in the right direction or making that all-important difference because the *power* of your work is being recognised.

You will then know that you have turned a corner and created a sense of fulfilment. For your contribution is now being noted by those around you, for they now comment on and acknowledge the difference you are making, which may in turn win others to your cause and therefore make an even bigger difference to the work world.

The opportunity to make a difference and heal the space centres on you in terms of what you value about your job, career or profession and in terms of what stirs you up. So in order to help you formulate your statements, try answering the following questions.

Questions to help you formulate your mission to heal the space

1 What is wrong with your job?

2 What is wrong with your profession?

3 What would you do in your job if you had more time?

4 What makes you feel angry about your job?

5 What make you feel really sad about your job?

6 What are you having to do in your job that you wish you weren't having to do?

7 If you had no restrictions on money, what would you do to make a real difference to the lives of others?

8 What would you really like to do that you haven't currently done to date?

9 If you knew the work world would reward you for your efforts, would you do it?

10 If you knew the work world would reward you far more than you are currently gaining, would you do it *now*?

Example

Your personal mission to heal the space

Now, it's time for you to write your mission. You need to make your mission real and true for you. Have a go at writing it down and see what comes up for you.

I value

I believe

I feel it is right to

In summary then

Whatever you love, you will do well. Creating a mission is to do what you love. Stand up for what you believe in and action what you feel is right and just. Remember, if you can do it you are truly on the way to rediscovering that elusive, missing and important piece of the jigsaw. A piece that will lead you to inner contentment and purpose. Take the plunge and do it. You will never look back again, for your future career is bright and joyous and has a newly defined purpose.

Step Six – Balance
Your Working Life
by Creating Simplicity
and Acceptance

Balance is crucial to your ability to actually enjoy your job. Do you feel in balance? Are you in balance some of the time but not at others? In short, do you give yourself permission to enjoy yourself?

Work has the capacity to complicate your life especially if:

- You are working 50–80 hours per week
- You have a difficult boss or colleagues
- You have a long way to commute
- You don't enjoy what you are doing at work
- You haven't the time to give to your spouse, children or home.

Work can, if you allow it to, encompass the whole of *you* and can therefore drain your capacity to give to your job, your family and most importantly yourself. It can also become a convenient excuse not to look at or confront the big questions. Questions such as:

- Am I really happy in my job?
- Am I getting too old for all this?
- Is time running out for me?
- Is it too late to change?
- Is work adversely affecting my health?
- What would I really like to be doing?

Work can also keep you busy because you may be 'trying to do it all' – to achieve that next promotion, next buzz, next bonus, next target, next goal or next title for either the boss, the organisation or yourself. The result is that you may be left feeling tired, drained, exhausted, flat, old, worn-out or even used. Drive, ambition and enthusiasm are key to success but there comes a point when you need to stop, pull back and re-evaluate where you are and where you want to go in your job. Otherwise your capacity to 'give' will gradually diminish as your work life gets fuller and fuller and then you may get out of balance.

When you are out of balance the capacity you have for fulfilling relationships at work and romantic love at home is substantially reduced. Hence even if you 'have it all' at the moment your capacity to see it and appreciate it will be blurred by your desire or need to strive for more and more. What is the solution if you don't want to drop out, are too young to retire or not in the financial position to do so anyway? What do you do if you have run out of ideas on how to solve the issue? The answer is to simplify your work and life outside of work.

Simplifying is therefore a perfect way to re-establish the balance. The first step is to establish what simplifying means to you, for it can be interpreted differently. For some it means:

- Not rushing to work
- Exploring new job options
- Achieving a balance between job and home life

- Cutting down on purchases
- Down-shifting to a smaller house or out of the city
- Selling a few possessions that are rarely used.

Whatever it is, it has to be meaningful to you but it usually involves a combination of some or all of the above, so that you can begin to get back 'in control of your working life'. Thus simplifying is all about letting go, perhaps of:

- Your need for power
- Your sense of importance
- Your ego
- Your feelings of achievement
- Your hyperactivity
- Your stress
- Your over-stimulation
- Your social engagements
- Your clutter
- Your need to 'have it all'.

And achieving a state of '*being*' rather than '*doing*'. By *being* more in a state of happiness, inner contentment and joy, you will realise you have the time, energy and space to have a really fulfilling time at work and at home. Simplifying, therefore, allows you to take work less seriously and have more quiet and meaningful times. Initially it is important that you establish what simplifying means to you. So have a go at answering the following four questions.

- What would you like to achieve by simplifying your work life?

- What would you like your job to look like?

- How will you know when you have got there?

- What can you change right now?

Ten easy steps to help you simplify your work within a month

Listed below are *ten* easy steps to help you simplify your work life within a month. The biggest thing you need to appreciate is that you don't have to work as hard as you might have led yourself to believe to date.

1. **Attract new people into your life.** Consider inviting new people into your life who don't perhaps work as hard as you do, and try to learn from them. They are there to help you achieve your new level of simplicity.
2. **Be willing to change.** If you are ready and willing to change, then change can happen. At this stage, you don't have to know

how and what you need to do; you just have to be prepared to explore the options. Make a habit of asking yourself every day for 30 days, 'What do I need to do to change?' Do you need to let go of your high expectations, your high standards and your high demands? Or is it more to do with control? Every day for 30 days ask yourself the same question and if possible write down what comes up. Then you can assess your list at the end of the 30-day period. Has one thing cropped up more than once? Were you surprised by what came up?

3 **Look at what you are holding on to.** For 30 days ask yourself, 'What am I holding on to in my job?' Again, note down on a piece of paper what comes up. Is it your power, your authority, your position, your level of respect, your sense of importance or the fact that you are needed? Let your thoughts come up and just note them down at this stage.

4 **Look at and notice all the things you think you should do.** For 30 days notice what tasks you are doing at work on automatic pilot without reflecting why you are doing them. Write them down and write next to them what you could do instead. Doing things automatically helps you to 'feel' in control but they also burden you at the same time. Try to change your responses.

5 **Look at what relationships you are running away from.** Work and heavy schedules mean that you lose sight of the importance of certain relationships. Be honest with yourself and for 30 days just notice which relationships you are running away from because you are too busy or working too hard. Is it your partner or spouse, your children, your boss, your colleagues or your clients?

6 **Look at what is feeding your ego.** What work situations or commitments are feeding your ego and desire to have or do more? Often you can take on too much or commit to things that are complicating your life. Have you any of these and, if so, what are they? Write them down.

7 **Look at how you could reduce your working day each day.** If your work has begun to creep into your free time, leisure time and weekends, now is the time to stop and look at how you can

reduce your working day by as little as ten minutes every day for a month. Then gradually, over the month, you will be working towards working your specified number of hours or contracted hours.

8 **Look at how you can communicate to your boss, colleagues and associates the fact that you are simplifying.** You may choose to get used to and feel comfortable with the simplification process before you communicate it to others. Or you may decide to tell others straightaway about your simplification programme. Whatever you decide, at some point you have to let people 'in' on the change in you as simplifying goes against the main grain of things.

9 **Look at how you can nourish your body.** Note down in the 30-day period how you intend to nourish your body better in terms of sleep, diet and exercise and how you intend to spend more time relaxing in nature or doing the things that you really enjoy.

10 **Look at how you can become less work-orientated.** Work is and can be a big disease. It forces people to stop laughing, forgiving and having fun. It creates, above all, a critical and over thinking generation of people. It creates people who lose their desire to be sensual and in touch with their thoughts, feelings and desires because there is always a job to do or a boss to be accountable to. Love, in effect, comes from the heart not the head because it brings you back in touch with yourself – a person who values what is real, right and what is important to you. A huge step towards achieving simplicity is to stop over-thinking about your job, your role and your responsibilities. For the over-thinking crams your brain full of ideas, concepts, thoughts, worries, feelings and concerns about things that may or may not happen. People who suffer from over-thinking are never at rest or at peace with where they find themselves. Calm or simplicity comes when you can stop the over-thinking and get to the point of 'this is it', right now – a point where you are more liberated, carefree and out of the regiment within your work life. For example, you may like to

be organised and tidy but on occasions allow yourself to be a little disorganised. You may pride yourself on being 'on time' but occasionally allow yourself to be a little late. You may pride yourself on being reliable but occasionally allow yourself to be a little unreliable. You can become less work-orientated without losing your ambition, drive and enthusiasm. You are you and are allowed to be less serious about work, and your work colleagues will appreciate you for it. Try to see the funny side of things. As you do this, a calmness and serenity will permeate your working life because your fears will dissolve. No longer will you be running through scenarios in your head. Notice the change in your energy as you move from a hectic, serious worker into a worker who can laugh, smile and enjoy work. As you step back from seriousness, work will turn from a struggle into a state of simplicity and balance. Just become aware of how you can drop your intensity about work and the need to 'be' or do everything.

When you are ready, try completing the following exercise as a sign of your commitment to yourself.

Your commitment to simplifying work

Nourishing your body
- What eating habits are you going to change?

- How are you going to restore your energy?

- What are you going to do to relax more?

- Are you willing to give your body the love and attention it deserves?

Work
- What working habits are you going to change (e.g. stop holding on to things, stop thinking you should do things)?

- How much are you going to reduce your working day by each day – ten, 15 or 20 minutes?

- How are you going to lighten up?

- What are you going to do to stop over-thinking about work?

Relationships

- What relationships are you going to work on – spouse, partner, children, boss, colleagues or clients?

- What are you going to improve?

- How are you going to do it?

Acceptance

Loving your job or work is directly linked to your ability to accept things. Acceptance is being grateful for how things are at the moment, rather than wishing that things could change or be different because this only encourages you to cover up or run away from the truth. True change comes from acceptance of how it is right now and an acceptance that it might take time to make the necessary changes or transitions.

People who love their work are both positive in terms of themselves and also in terms of others. They are people who really appreciate what others do for them and they appreciate their world, their circumstances and of course, their job. As a result they attract even more good into their working lives. In fact, these upbeat people are often described, through many people's gritted teeth, as 'Being *so* nice!' Be honest with yourself, how many times did you feel grateful for things last week?

Do you like it when others make a fuss of you? Do you like

STEP SIX – BALANCE YOUR WORKING LIFE

being thanked for a job well done? Do you like being rewarded? Most people don't just love to be acknowledged and fussed; they crave it! It's no fun for people going to bed at night feeling unsure about themselves or even feeling unappreciated. So, in order to break this habit, you need to start looking at your work with 'new and loving eyes' and bringing more love into your working life.

- How many people can you smile at?
- How may people around you are helping you to do something right now?
- How many people need a phone call to say Hi?
- How many people are important to you at work?
- How many things do you take for granted?
- How many people have you said 'Thank you' to this week?

In the 'small' and 'simple' you will find the 'great' and, yes, that sense of fulfilment.

By looking at your job today, as if for the first time, you will be amazed by what you have missed or taken for granted – the roof over your head; fresh, clean running water; heat and lighting; transport to work; telecommunications; the furniture; the stationery; the view from the window; the friendly colleagues; the refreshment facilities; the building; the environment and the day ahead. Being appreciative and grateful is addictive – others will respond to you better and make your day all the more enjoyable. Being grateful also gives you a huge boost in energy, love and freedom.

Gratitude also helps you decrease your dependence on 'things'. It is no longer the job that has to make you happy; it is no longer the outcome or the end result; it is *you* and the way you react along the way. You are no longer making a contract with your job, such as 'Give me this or else!', which is just a desperate plea to become even more important, powerful and successful. Therefore if possible *avoid*:

- Trying to control any situation or person
- Trying to show another person how it 'should' be done
- Trying to impress your boss, colleagues and staff
- Trying to get your own way
- Trying to be better than everyone else.

In all of these lies the struggle between you and work. Choose to approach your job as an area in which to cultivate yourself and be grateful for all your messages about areas that need to be improved. Give up what has to be given up, prune what has to be pruned and strive without embarrassment or apology. Then and only then will work change from being a chore and a difficult time into a time of learning about your necessary development.

However, although in principle it is an easy and simple process it can be a 'tough' concept for some people to accept, mainly because they get caught up in self-protection or self-justification rather than accepting the 'truth' and thereby doing something about amending or resolving the situation.

For example, in one of my group training sessions I had a member of the group who became quite agitated about one of the questionnaires he had filled in. His answers highlighted that he was more comfortable being part of a group than leading the group. He was adamant that this was wrong, for his whole job was about leading and directing a group of people. When I asked him, 'What part of the answer don't you like?' he became hot and agitated and said, 'The answer is wrong as it says that I am not suited to my role.' I pointed out that he had provided the answer to the question and asked what he didn't like about it. He still felt that 'I was wrong' and that 'I had got it all wrong' and that 'I shouldn't have written that'. I again reminded him that he had provided the answer to the question. I asked him whether he had ever stepped aside or away from a group because he felt uncomfortable or unhappy about making an unpopular decision.

He replied, 'Yes, I do sometimes but not often.'

I then asked him, 'So is your answer correct?'

He replied, 'Yes, it is, but I don't like the fact that it has been revealed.'

Great, so we had got there at last. The truth about being aware of his weakness was horribly uncomfortable for him, more uncomfortable than talking about how he could take on the leadership role within tricky situations by asking himself power questions and waiting for the answers rather than withdrawing from the situation altogether.

Hence this example demonstrates how acceptance can be a hurdle for some people, as they may not want to work through the solution. If you can accept and recognise the truth then you will be more willing to accept your personal development to date and thereby work on developing the highlighted areas.

Step Seven – Appreciating, Understanding and Releasing the *Real* You

The last chapter of this book is about getting to know yourself again and releasing *more* of yourself at work. Knowing exactly who you are and what you need to learn is the only solution to any job issue – without it you will never really get out of the 'pain cycle' because on some level you think that you have nothing left to learn, develop or improve.

You probably think that you know yourself pretty well already and you do. You know what you like doing and what you are good at but it is impossible to truly know all of yourself until such a time as you know, accept and are addressing your shortcomings and negative habits on a regular basis. Believing you have nothing left to learn will encourage you to keep yourself comfortable and put off the necessity to look at yourself. Unless you accept your incompleteness and your lack of perfection, you slowly begin to lose your capacity to develop and have job fulfilment.

As you feel less fulfilled by your job, do you rely more upon judgment, accusations and criticisms as was perhaps highlighted by the self-development questionnaire in Step Three. For example, have you ever been in a staff meeting or in a conversation with someone where your colleague is pinpointing an issue as another person's failure to listen, and you are literally amazed? Amazed because you would have said exactly the same thing about the colleague making the accusation? Often people see themselves as exactly the opposite of how they are, because the image they have of themselves deceives them into believing the opposite of what they want to believe is true.

So what is the solution? People are often brought face to face with their shortcomings. This means that they may get picked up in their appraisals, staff meetings or by other colleagues about, for example, their lack of listening skills. The self-concept is so deeply personal to people that it can hurt, embarrass, shame, anger or upset the person if they feel they are being criticised or if they feel someone is suggesting they are not the person they feel themself to be. Sadly, it is common for people to remain 'stuck' in their justification of themselves, their habits or in their attempt to get even. It is, however, far more powerful to recognise the 'truth' and to do something about amending it.

So you have to become more self-aware and self-amending. Instead of deceiving yourself about who you think you are, you have to really acquire and work upon the skills that you think you have and need to acquire, in order to become 'more' in terms of an employee or worker. If you believe you listen well, do it. If you believe you are a good timekeeper, then show up on time. Equally, if you believe you are positive, note how many positive comments you make in a day in relation to negative ones, and work on increasing the positive ones and decreasing the negative ones.

The one purpose behind everything in the work world is to see *yourself* and to keep looking until you see it all – the good stuff and the not-so-good stuff! As soon as you start to look at yourself, you have started the biggest search of all – the search for you and for your lost or forgotten dreams or hopes and how you can become more fulfilled at work.

Discovering more about you

Your image of yourself is made up of three parts, namely the 'ideal self', 'self-image' and 'self-esteem'.

The 'ideal self' is, as the name suggests, the person you would like to be. It is your idea of what makes up a 'sparky' person and it is based upon your early programming, beliefs, attitudes and, of course, job experiences.

The second part, of 'self-image', is your image in terms of how you think of yourself. How would you describe yourself to others in terms of looks and behaviour? How do you present yourself to others in terms of your dress style, vocabulary and manners? It is important to point out that many people see themselves in terms of how others see them. For example, a person might only regard themself as hardworking, special or successful if it is noticed and commented on by others. So how dependent are you upon other people's opinions, views and approval of you? Do you care what others think of you? Do you do what you want to do regardless of what others might say, do or think, or do you check things out beforehand? This is crucial to your development of job fulfilment. Many people remain trapped inside themselves because they have got so used to listening, taking in and acting upon an outsider's opinion or view of themselves. This is different from appointing someone to be a mentor or advisor because such a person would be fulfilling a positive role, whereas an outsider may not have your interests at heart!

Having the job that you want does involve doing what you want to do, so be aware that it is vitally important that you begin to drop your dependence on others. Sure, they may not like it very much, especially in the beginning, because they have got used to giving their views and advice or having their say. Let's face it, it probably made them feel very important and perhaps even a bit powerful. More importantly, though, it has stopped you from doing what you really wanted and, of course, moving forward. Aside from all that, it didn't help your 'advisor' either because it lulled them into thinking that they no longer needed to develop themself further. Watch out, though; if you take responsibility for yourself and drop your need to check back, refer and ask advice, your 'advisors' may get angry, critical or resistant towards you. You can deal with that by accepting that their negative reactions won't last long as they begin to see the 'new you', the person who is now happy to take full responsibility for themself.

By taking the initiative and control you are showing and allowing others, especially your 'advisors', to do the same for themselves too. To keep up the momentum of change and development, list three things that you are going to work on for 30 days in order to avoid the temptation to revert to your old ways. Rejecting other people's image of you is by far the most positive thing you can do for yourself and it opens up that box inside you called '*desire*' again and closes the one called '*dependency*'. What two other things could you change? Perhaps criticising others, asking for approval or begging for compliments. Start instead to become your own coach and listen to your own daily needs and desires.

The third part of your image of yourself is 'self-esteem', or how you feel about yourself. As a child you were not often in a position to decide for yourself, so you 'owned' and relied upon other people's view of you. Those repeated messages, which you received day-in and day-out about you, now determine how good you feel about yourself. So if you were lucky enough to receive positive or constructive comments, then the majority of your beliefs about yourself will be helping you now. If, on the other hand, you were unfortunate to have received a continual stream of negative comments, such as being told 'not to do something', 'to always ask for help' or 'to stop trying', then you are likely to have formed many barriers that will stop you believing that you can do certain things or have what you want and deserve now.

As an adult, you are free to make your own choices and, whereas in the past your boss, colleagues, associates, clients or customers may have told you otherwise, now it is your time to decide for yourself. Initially it may not appear to be so. But consider this concept: if everything you do now was something you learnt in the past – whether your reaction to that is a positive response or a negative one – in effect all you have to do now is to unlearn the negative habits and change the response from negative to positive.

Fear

Fear is the biggest single barrier that will prevent you from achieving any level of passion, excitement or fulfilment from your job. If you let it, fear will stop you from looking at yourself or having any job fulfilment long-term.

However, fear itself is an extremely positive thing. Fear stops you from tripping up, alerts you to any potential dangers and often prevents you from making a fool of yourself. But sadly so many people actually get used to living in a state of fear or anxiety that it is almost as if the fears can't bear to keep quiet. Do your fears manage you or is it the other way round?

Your fears will, if you allow them to, constantly remind you of this and that. Fear will remind you of what might happen in the future, if you do or don't do something at work. Your fears will also remind you of what you didn't complete or finish off yesterday, of that time when you did too much, or of what you should be or could be doing right now, this minute. In fact, your fears, anxieties and worries will keep you so busy that you could find yourself worrying all, if not most, of the time and then even worrying about worrying. Worry and fear have to be kept in check, otherwise you'll have no time left to do or enjoy the job and work life you have created for yourself.

Although worry is natural, it needs to be managed appropriately; otherwise it'll manage you. Next time you find yourself worrying about your work, for example, about what you have to do or what you haven't done, just note it and, if it is unimportant, bin it; if it is important try thanking the thought and decide when you'll do what has just occurred to you. Usually the thought will go away as it now has an answer about *when* it'll be done. It is then up to you to do it at a time of your choosing, otherwise the fear thought will be back.

It is also important to remember that fears are only thoughts which can be managed and resolved. Most people tend to build upon their fears so that they get bigger and bigger but in reality it is only the mind's way of getting your attention and telling you to do something about resolving the fear thought. Try to remain in control by managing your fears and thoughts and then you can enjoy the 'present' moment much more.

Putting things off

As mentioned earlier, most people try to put off becoming self-aware. Why? Very often because they are either afraid about what they may discover or they are afraid they might have to change something. As a result they put off doing it because they may decide they are too busy or tired, or feel that it has to be done properly or perfectly by someone professional. There is never a perfect time to start, so now is as good a time as any to get started. Brace yourself and choose to discover what you've always wanted to know – who you really are and what skills you need to develop.

Past mistakes

The fear of revealing past mistakes can form a big barrier for many people and this in itself can affect a person's view of the present, past and future. Your work mistakes offer you a great insight into your future job development. It is important to bear in mind that it is often not the mistake that affects you but your own reaction to it or how you perceived that someone else reacted to your mistake. Try to avoid reliving the past as it only makes it feel real for you in the present. Is it therefore time to drop the past and to perhaps either try again or do something to amend or overcome the mistake? Your first step is to change the word 'mistake' into a 'result'. This helps it be less personal and helps you decide whether you wish to do something about amending the result.

Attitude

The importance of your attitude cannot be underestimated. In fact your attitude affects whether you like your job, whether you get on with your colleagues, whether you are likely to be well-liked, respected and valued and above all whether you progress in your job or stay where you are at present. Whether you like it or not, work is merely a reflection of *you* and your attitude.

If you have a negative, pessimistic and hard-done-by attitude, you are likely to attract experiences that confirm this state of mind. If, on the other hand, you have a happy, relaxed, committed, purposeful and hardworking attitude, you are likely to attract more positive work experiences into your life. The work world doesn't really care whether you succeed or are fulfilled or not, but you do. Your attitude not only affects you but it also affects your colleagues and associates. However, it is not just a matter of developing a happy, smiley grin. People can see through this and will regard you with caution as they 'pick up' on the fact that there is no sincerity present. Cultivating a good attitude is about meaning what you say, doing what you promise and by caring about yourself and others. Your workmates and colleagues want to be treated with respect, compassion and above all importance – they want to feel recognised, needed and valued too, so if you can satisfy both their needs and your own needs, your circumstances and experiences will dramatically change for the better.

To sum up

To sum up this section on 'discovering more about you', it is important to remember that you tend to see things not as they are, but as you are. By understanding yourself better and by working on yourself daily you are encouraging and developing positive emotions and experiences for yourself. Part of the process of 'getting what you want out of your job' is to become the sort of person you'd like to be. Begin the process and notice the difference. Wonderfully, as soon as you begin the process of really becoming self-aware and searching for what is important to you, your quest for job fulfilment has been activated. Try completing the following exercises on self-awareness to help you know, appreciate and understand what might be holding you back from feeling really good about your current job and prospects.

Your ideal self, self-image and self-esteem

Fill in the chart below and be as honest as possible with yourself. Write down everything that comes up, however significant or insignificant it may appear at the time.

The ideal self
- How would you like to be regarded in your job?

- What do you need in order to achieve that?

Self-image
- Describe as briefly as you can your image in terms of dress style, appearance, attitude, vocabulary and behaviour.

- How much do you rely on other people's opinions, ideas and thoughts?

- What do you feel you lack?

Self-esteem
- How do you feel about yourself?

- How positive was your childhood/early adulthood?

- What beliefs about yourself may be hindering your development?

- On a scale of one to 100, how positive are you at work?

STEP SEVEN – RELEASING THE *REAL* YOU

You and your fear

Again fill in the chart below with as much detail as possible.

- What is your biggest worry about work?

- Has it ever happened and, if so, how often?

- What could you have done to resolve or change the circumstances?

- What were you worrying about last year?

- Is that important today?

- What worries you about next year?

- Will that be important in five years' time?

- What choices are open to you to help yourself right now?

- What fears are you going to drop today?

- What positive thoughts are going to replace your fears?

You and your resistance

Complete and fill in the chart below:

- What do you put off doing at work?

- How often do you put things off?

- What is the reason you give?

- What are you afraid you might discover?

- What have you missed out on?

- How willing are you to try something new and exciting?

You and your work attitude

Complete and fill in the chart below:

What is going to be your attitude to work from now on:

- Flexible
- Willing
- Committed
- Fun
- Positive
- Enthusiastic

- Flowing
- Progressive
- Creative
- Thorough
- Exciting
- Open-minded
- Other attitudes of your choosing _____

- How would your colleagues describe you at present?

- How are you going to change?

- How often are you prepared to work on your attitude – daily, weekly or yearly?

- How well-liked are you?

- How do your colleagues respond to you when you enter a room? Are they friendly, warm and enthusiastic or are they more aloof, distant and negative?

• What are you going to change?

Building your view of yourself

It's been said many times before but no real 'spark' about your job is possible unless you 'like' yourself. Cultivate a habit of liking yourself and developing a sense of self-respect, self-awareness and self-confidence.

To do this, choose *five* of your key strengths and qualities to acknowledge and *five* of your negative habits you are willing to work on.

List five key qualities and strengths	
The quality	How does it help you in your work?
1	
2	
3	
4	
5	

List five habits you are willing to work on	
Habit	How you are going to work upon it?
1	
2	
3	
4	
5	

Releasing yourself

Eight ways to release yourself

Listed below are eight things to help you release yourself. These will help you to use your energy, enthusiasm and efforts creatively and also to stay on track when you don't want to do something, feel tired or maybe a little disillusioned.

1 Goals

Feeling good about your job and your work contribution isn't something you can buy or acquire instantly, so you need carefully and clearly to define your goals. Much of this work has been done already in terms of defining what you want more of, what causes you to lose energy and what you need to do in terms of building your self-image. Next, you need to decide what you are going to work on first, when are going to do it and for how long. It is far better, for example, to do half an hour each day if you can, rather than half a day at the weekend. Do you have work-related goals? Are they written down? How often do you refer to them? How long-term are your goals? Are your goals specific and tangible? Do you know exactly what you have to do to achieve your goals? What are you currently working upon?

Goals are your personal objectives and they represent your 'love' of your job. If your goals are weak, then your feelings about your job will chop and change and you may have a rollercoaster ride through work. However, if your goals are forceful, honest, direct, tangible and passionate then your commitment to your job is strong and you will be able to ride any setbacks or hurdles. How strong and passionate are your goals? Do your goals act as a commitment to yourself that you actually need 'something' from your job? Do they help you to visualise, imagine and ultimately create what it is that would give you satisfaction?

Time is a big hurdle in terms of goals, for many people view time as an opportunity to say, 'I haven't got time to do that.' The reality is there is a price to pay for having a fantastic job and that price is the fact that you are going to have to create that love for your job. And in creating your dream job you may have to sacrifice a few things along the way.

If you are working then your free time is precious. How do you use your spare time at present? Is it effective or do you waste a lot of free time? In order to achieve your goals and find that passion for your job again, you need to re-evaluate how you use your leisure time every day if you are to make it 'all' happen. If you are not prepared to do this, then your desire for a great job isn't strong enough. For goals are only achieved by sheer determination and commitment, not by half-heartedness. Sure, it sounds hard and tough but every stop, every excuse and every break is a reason for you to give up and to put up with things as they are at present. Keep your mind on the goal, not on what you are giving up, not doing or missing out on. Keep the focus on your goal, 'How do I make this job of mine even more fantastic?'

2 Desire

Your desire is crucial to improving your job situation. Do you feel jealous and frustrated that others have a better job than you? These so-called 'other people' are your greatest inspiration so make them your icons and allow your feelings of jealousy and frustration to disappear. Spur yourself on and ensure you refuel your desire. Please don't be disillusioned into thinking that if you ignore your feelings they will go away of their own accord, because hiding your feelings or ignoring them doesn't work. All it means is that they may go away for a while but they will usually crop up even stronger next time around. So even though 'the person with the fabulous job' is very close to you stop, slow down and rejoice because there it is right in front of you. Instead of huffing, moaning and complaining about it, have a look at it.

- What is it about the great job that you want?
- How does the individual concerned look on the great job?
- How many hours are they working?
- How much time off do they have?
- Does their work look easy?

Try to pinpoint what it is exactly that is irritating you, making your blood boil or creating that jealous feeling because they have what you want. Desire is all about feeling passionate about something. If you build on your feelings and determine how you can turn them around, then you are truly on your way to getting more from your job too.

3 Patience

'Having it all', which is what having a great job will give you, also involves being patient. Patience is about developing a sense of timing and consistency. It is about having a goal and working at it rather than rushing at it. Now it is easy to say that patience is what is required but the truth is, do you rush at things and get frustrated if things don't happen quickly enough?

Many, many job problems are actually relationship problems.

For example, other people don't listen to what you have said and they hijack the conversation, turning it around to ensure they achieve the best result for themselves. It is at times like these that patience is needed because whether you like it or not, the work world is run on relationships and it is never good to fall out with another individual. Hurt pride or a wounded ego are negative feelings and can affect the way you feel about yourself, so try to develop a more relaxed and patient approach towards others. If nothing else, it will help you to keep your positive energy levels up and your own ego intact.

4 Be realistic
Being realistic is about being kind to yourself. You need to ask yourself some tough questions when you have set your goals. Ask yourself these questions as if they were someone else's goals.

- Is this goal realistic or does it need to be broken down into smaller bits?
- What about the timescale of the goal, is that realistic too?

A colleague told me once at our Christmas dinner that her New Year's resolution was to become less perfect next year. Initially after the shock of the word 'perfect', I asked her to explain what she meant. She explained that she often felt stressed because she had such high standards for herself and always wanted things to be just so. She was taking a whole year over working with this one issue because, as she put it, 'I don't want to be too hard on myself or to put myself under any more pressure.'

So your goals have to be appropriate to you. Also bear in mind that you might have to enlist the support or the mentoring skills of another person in order to help you overcome any mental hurdles or obstacles you may have. Can you identify anyone?

5 Overcoming hurdles

There are hurdles, barriers and obstacles around every corner. They are there to allow you to see how you are doing and discover how committed you are to bypassing, going round or jumping over them. However, many people allow these hurdles to get the better of them, perhaps because they need a rest, a break or a chance to reflect.

At the end of this chapter there is a sheet for you to complete that will become your reminder and your commitment to putting the passion back in your job. On this sheet you are asked to put down what you think your biggest obstacles or hurdles will be. By acknowledging and admitting that you have some, you can then think about what you can do to overcome each one.

Often people create obstacles because on some level they don't feel that they deserve the thing they desire so they either mess up the process or put a stop to it. But by allowing yourself to receive, you are allowing for *more* good things and good experiences to find their way to you. Open your door and all you have to say is 'thank you'.

6 Enjoy change

Change is a big subject and much has been written about it in recent years. Whether you like change, hate it or just put up with it, change is what this book is all about. No one actually stays put or stands still for long, although you may think you do. If change is managed and directed positively, it can become fun and exciting rather than scary and frightening. Let's take a closer look at the change cycle.

Anyone can change or improve any aspect of their job or career. All it takes is the realisation that change is desirable, coupled with realistic expectations and a degree of sensible planning. By going through the process of self-analysis you have already begun the change process. Initially when you analyse yourself, because you may feel uncomfortable with it, you may try to work out what is 'wrong'. But hopefully you have discovered that this is a positive process, not a reason to beat yourself up and that you are now *ready* to take that all-important step to self-improvement and self-development.

Perhaps it is time for you to move on or simply to stop repeating the same things over and over again. Ideally you can now log the problems or issues as they occur at work and work out what needs to change and what needs to be done to stop it from happening again.

Most people, if they are honest, really want change – either a change in themselves or a change in their circumstances. Change is all part of self-esteem and contentment but this does not mean that the process will be easy for you, or needs to be difficult for that matter. All it really means is that you need to select the right things to change and choose the right way to go about it. In other words, you need to become comfortable with the process of change itself.

Is there an element of psychological conservatism in you? Are you conservative on your behalf and also on behalf of others? Do you try to cocoon yourself in a web of cosy familiarity at work in which you carry out your activities and duties? Do you feel threatened if others, namely your colleagues or subordinates, rebel against the roles in which you have cast them?

If achieving your goal means changing your style or approach, it is a good idea to let people in on the secret; that way you are less likely to be deflected or tripped up by any hurdles or obstacles they may erect in your path. Remember my colleague; she let me in on her secret, perhaps because she didn't want to receive any negative comments on her seeming lack of perfection or sloppy standards all of a sudden!

Before setting up a programme of change, it is essential to get to know yourself. Hence the preceding exercises. And, of course, establish just how much you want it – for change never works as well if you are merely yielding to someone else's demands or needs.

Above all, it is important not to passively accept others' views of you. How can anyone really know what you are capable of? You are not certain yourself so they can only guess at your determination to improve. The best sort of change is self-generated and self-motivated. How then is change brought about? The process of change has five phases, which you have to pass through on the way to achieving your goals and completing your mission to creating more enthusiasm about your job.

Phase 1 – the honeymoon period
The phase of euphoria when you know where you want to go and you concentrate on all the positive aspects of what you are doing and forget the rest.

Phase 2 – the identity crisis
The phase of self-doubt when you ask yourself disturbing and tricky questions. What was wrong with the way I used to be anyway? Am I really up to this? Is this worth it? Why didn't anyone tell me this was going to be so difficult? Nothing is going right. Why is no one helping or telling me what to do?

Phase 3 – the trough
You are facing a decision. There are only two ways out of this. Go back to the old ways or press on with renewed determination.

Phase 4 – the breakthrough
This is the experience you get when suddenly, after all your hard work, everything clicks into place. It usually happens after a period when you have been working on yourself and have perhaps endured a bit of pain or had a real struggle and suddenly you get a big insight. This insight will significantly change the way you see yourself and the way you choose to work. For example, these insights may give you:

- a vision of what is possible in the future
- a feeling of liberation from your everyday worries, fears and concerns
- a feeling of possibility and freedom.

It is usually tricky for a person to tell or recount their experience to another. For what may be a momentary flash of inner knowing may at the time seem like a lifetime. For in this experience and insight all the little pieces of the jigsaw just slip effortlessly into place. Also it is the taking away of the everyday efforts, struggles and doubts that make this experience all the more exceptional, beautiful and amazing. So, although it may be a short experience time-wise, the strength and meaning of it may be timeless.

Breakthrough experiences tend to be as a result of much effort and hard work on the part of the individual. It is not dissimilar to a tap dripping water into a cup. Initially it seems impossible that these few drops will fill the cup up but gradually, bit by bit, the cup begins to fill up until such a time as it spills over the top. The overflow represents the breakthrough. It is symbolic because it is a sign to say that the real work starts now, for you are full. Your tank and inner vessels will still need to be kept topped up, though, and looked after, but you are now in a position to help others and to heal the space.

Many people understandably get caught up in the moment itself, for it makes them feel the best they have felt in a long time, and they often want that feeling back again and again. They often seek or work upon trying to gain another insight. There is no real doubt as to why this happens because breakthroughs do truly make you feel full of yourself, your potential and capabilities and that is something to savour. It can, however, also be addictive. In reality these 'peak experiences', as they are often called, are the beginning, not the end. These experiences are a sign that you are in fact ready to start giving in earnest and not that everything is complete for you.

Breakthroughs may enable you to:

- See the past patterns
- See the past mistakes
- Visualise the future
- Have a greater understanding of things

- Put things into perspective
- Feel you've 'got it' at long last.

The feeling of 'I've got it' is common. On the one hand, it can make you feel truly great and full of energy and vitality. On the other hand, it can make you feel cross or angry with the rest of the world because they don't appear to have got it yet.

At this stage of the cycle be warned, though; you may begin to view others negatively, perhaps as slow, dead or boring. It is often this distrust, dislike or frustration with the rest of the work world that can disillusion you. Having an insight is fantastic because it gives you great vision, but that is all. It doesn't give you a licence to criticise others that in your view may still be asleep. If you do then you have done what is often described as 'dropping the sword'. 'Dropping the sword' is dangerous because the focus is on you and how wonderful you are, and not on what your contribution or giving is all about. There is always a danger that your vision becomes too big for you to carry, too tricky or maybe you begin to doubt it, and it is at this time when you may want to get cross with the work world, perhaps because no one else around you has 'got it' or appears to want it. Encourage yourself, however, to continue the climb, for there is further to go; you can still make it alone and others will join you later.

It is important to realise that you may have had a vision or insight to shake you up and to stir you into action. Remember that the onus is on *you*, you alone, to do something.

The final hurdle is to surrender to your insight and new knowledge and not fight it, control it or to try to recreate it because that will only lead to disappointment. People often feel that if they 'let go' they'll end up like the people they despise or hate. Work, it is true, has a big 'pull' on most people. It pulls you in each day and, if you are not careful, it can also pull you to do what others do. As a result, you can begin to lose your identity. Surrender doesn't mean giving it up or throwing it away but it does mean letting the rest take care of itself. All you have to do is to make that all-important commitment to yourself. A commitment of behaving in a way that you are proud of and giving to your job. You don't have to start too big. Be kind to yourself and start small and build up. Begin with the everyday sort of things like:

• Being nice to people
• Respecting others
• Trying to understand things from someone else's perspective
• Looking for the good in others
• Being slow to judge
• Putting yourself out
• Avoiding office gossip and back-stabbing
• Being tolerant to others
• Being patient and kind
• And learning to forgive.

You can have the big experiences and the big breakthroughs by beginning with and working on the smaller stuff. Little by little, being kind to yourself and others changes you in a big way because it is not temporary and it not a quick win. Instead of thinking, 'How do I go back and work after I have experienced or seen this?', try to go back with a sense of excitement and wonder.

Imagine for a moment what you have been missing and not doing to date. A new and wonderful chance awaits you and you must reach for it. You are now ready, able and equipped to 'give back' to yourself and others what you already have and know. Stick with it, keep on target and you will achieve your goal.

Phase 5 – 'back from the dead'

This is the point at which you realise that you are on the right road, that you are becoming comfortable with your new way of being and are happy and confident with who you are and what you are doing work-wise.

It is worth bearing in mind that significant change never happens overnight and progress is rarely smooth. Stopping too soon is one of the major reasons for failure, being deterred by temporary setbacks is another. You need to be prepared for a few tricky phases and be aware that if there is no resistance or struggle there is no real or significant change happening. Success hinges on the right attitude and guarding yourself against your excuses or pessimism.

7 Reward yourself

Don't forget to reward yourself for your efforts. Recognise what you have achieved and celebrate your successes. This is a long process and many people simply give up or lose interest in creating the job of their dreams because it all feels like too much hard work. Protect yourself against this by building in a reward system. Promise yourself a treat each week if you attain your target and keep that promise. It may be a present to yourself, some time off perhaps or a trip somewhere, whatever motivates you to keep going.

8 Put it on paper

Finally, before you start the change process, make your commitment concrete by writing it down. When it is there on paper in front of you, it is somehow much more real and difficult to walk away from. It is also much easier to share with your boss, colleagues and clients. Write it down and pin it on the wall or stick it on your desk or computer where you can see it every day. It will help you and help reinforce your commitment and desire. *Let's write it now!*

My commitment to putting the love back into my job

* My mission is to:

- My goal/s in terms of loving my job is/are to:

- The major benefit I will get from achieving my goal(s) is to:

- The things that are currently preventing me from achieving my goal(s) are:

- I am going to overcome these by:

- This is how long it will take me to achieve my goal(s):

- This is how I am going to do it:

- Daily targets:

- Weekly targets   Reward for success:

- Monthly targets   Reward for success:

- I will know I have achieved my goal(s) when:

- When I have achieved my goal(s) I feel:

Conclusion

The love test

Now the big one. You have filled in many questionnaires and completed many mind-provoking exercises in this book. It is now time to put yourself to the test, the love test, and see just how you feel about your job now that you have completed the book.

		Yes	No
1	Are you *more* aware of what job fulfilment means to you?	Yes	No
2	Are you more aware of what is causing you to lose your energy?	Yes	No
3	Are you more aware of what you want, in terms of your job and career?	Yes	No
4	Are you willing to take positive action to implement your needs and desires?	Yes	No
5	Are you more willing to make more of an effort to be positive?	Yes	No

6　Are you willing to take a stand in terms   Yes   No
of your personal mission to 'heal the
space'?

7　Are you willing to show more gratitude   Yes   No
towards your colleagues, workmates,
staff and everyone you come into
contact with?

8　Are you willing to be more flexible in   Yes   No
terms of becoming more focused on the
process than having to have a certain
result?

9　Are you more committed towards   Yes   No
creating the 'spark' in your job
rather than expecting it to happen?

10　Are you willing to have more fun and   Yes   No
laughs and adopt a lighter hearted
approach to work?

11　Are you willing to change more things   Yes   No
in your life, perhaps the way you get to
work, what you read or listen to on the
way and what you do for lunch?

12　Are you more persistent in your approach   Yes   No
to your job?

13　Are you willing to be more forgiving and   Yes   No
to allow yourself and others to make
mistakes, to slip up or to change
direction a bit?

14 Are you more aware of how to build up your self-image, self-awareness and self-esteem?	Yes	No
15 Are you willing to create balance in terms of your job?	Yes	No
16 Are you feeling more empowered now than before reading the book?	Yes	No
17 Do you feel that success or job fulfilment is more achievable now than before?	Yes	No
18 Are you willing to write down your plans and goals?	Yes	No
19 Are you willing to stick to them?	Yes	No
20 Are you willing to reward yourself for your progress to date?	Yes	No

Did you answer 'Yes' to every question? I sincerely hope so, because if you did you are well on your way to creating exactly what you want from your job. Good luck with your new approach. Be strong and remember, the *little* things in life really do make a big difference.

At some point in your career you do need to stop and take an inventory of who you are and what you have done. This fearless searching of yourself not only focuses on what you have done wrong and on the things you wish you had done in a different way, but it also focuses on the most important aspect of all, which is what you have done well, right and what you could be 'more of' in terms of your strengths and capabilities.

Being honest with yourself is about appreciating the good, powerful, creative, loving and compassionate part of yourself.

When you stop and acknowledge what you have been and done and are working on, you are on the path to becoming 'more' of what you already are. Enjoy your job, spark up your profession and give to all the people that you meet within your daily activities.

Case studies

This section is about some of the people with whom I have had the pleasure of working in either one-to-one or group career consultancy sessions to help them create more purpose, fulfilment or spark from their job or work. Each session has offered a unique insight into people's experiences, lives and aspirations for the future.

All sessions have provided a great opportunity to help people work through issues, rebuild long-lost dreams and plan their road ahead. Throughout the sessions my clients begin to 'shine' as they once again begin to recognise and acknowledge their vital and important contribution to the work world. It is this renewed sense of self-belief and self-recognition that provides clients with the impetus to make any necessary changes and internal shifts.

Case study 1: A property manager

A property manager who was on a three-month notice period used the consultancy sessions to change his attitude and behaviour and in doing so saved his job with his current organisation. When this client arrived for his first two sessions he was half an hour late. The client never took ownership for his late arrivals as he blamed the traffic, my directions and even his car. The client's lack of promptness and list of excuses conveyed a lot to me in terms of hidden feelings. At the beginning of session three, I raised the issue and the client became defensive and angry. Facing the truth about his current circumstances and feelings was a big issue for this client. He had to admit that he was angry with his employer about the redundancy notice, he felt scared about the prospect of finding another job within such a short space of time and he also felt angry with himself. When had it all gone pear-shaped? Was he to blame? And could he have prevented this? He talked through everything that was coming up, including the things he liked about his current job, such as the image, profile and prestige of the company, and also the things he didn't like, such as time pressure and deadlines.

Although he admitted that he had asked the company to provide help for him, he did resent the fact that he had to turn up to meet me on time and he didn't enjoy doing the preparation work between sessions. Once he started to admit that he had all sorts of different feelings and emotions that left him feeling tired, old and heavy he could start to unlock himself from protecting himself, his feelings and his pride.

The self-development questionnaire helped him to begin to focus on his strengths of loyalty, kindness, empathy and the needs of the customer. He began to realise that the pressures of the job had stopped him from focusing outwards. He began to accept that he needed to speak up for himself at work and to express how he felt. He worked out ways in which he could say what he wanted to say without coming across as rude or aggressive. This had been his pattern in the past, partly due to the fact that he kept things bottled up for too long and then they just spilled out.

All in all the sessions helped the client to soften and value himself and his job. Although he was actively job-seeking and attending interviews, his employer offered him a 'second chance' because his employer valued what he had done to improve his attitude and approach. He accepted a new job with his old organisation.

Case study 2: A sales and marketing manager

A sales and marketing manager who worked in the family-owned and -run business used the consultancy sessions to create the belief that he was worth 'more' in terms of money, recognition and status. His role within the family business was literally draining him of his energy and commitment, for he had to refer every decision back to his father-in-law. The business set-up and the family issues were constricting and constraining him. He no longer felt of value or recognised for his contribution and felt starved in terms of income. A change of direction raised doubts and fears about how the family would react and whether he could secure a job, which he felt he was worth even though his current salary didn't reflect that.

This client recognised that although he wanted to step forward and take action he didn't feel ready for it. A lot of work was done in the belief section so that this client could begin to rely on himself and not look outside for other people's approval. So new beliefs had to be created that reflected that the client valued and recognised himself. This client also had to spend time building his own energy on a day-to-day basis because he knew that he had to be strong when facing up to the family about doing what he wanted to do. He took the time to do his preparation beforehand and only when he felt ready did he apply for jobs. He secured himself a great job, doubled his salary and managed to 'stay in' with the family.

Case study 3: A creative designer

This designer was facing a job crisis in terms of his current job not fulfilling him but he was feeling terrified about stepping out and going it alone. He was working incredibly long hours and was restricted in terms of what he could and couldn't do design-wise. This client was tired of feeling undervalued, underpaid and tired of his face-to-face confrontations with his boss. His weekends and holidays kept him sane and also provided him with the opportunity to build up a client base.

The self-development questionnaire helped him to see his patterns of behaviour, and the questions on 'creating your personal mission' helped him to realise and accept that he still had a burning ambition to be able to give of himself and his skills to his job. So his big questions were, 'Am I ready to set up in business? Is being self-employed for me?'

This client had to spend time looking at his beliefs about work and his beliefs about money. Although he felt vulnerable in letting go of many of his old beliefs about money he felt it was time to build up a new image and profile for himself. He began to value and recognise his unique design skills and expertise, and looked at how he could use these as a foundation for a business. His wife's skills of sales, marketing and accounting helped to complete the jigsaw. Plans were made to create the new business. Seven years later he describes his consultancy sessions as, 'The best investment decision I ever made'. He never confesses to being a great businessman but he wins contracts and attracts big clients on the basis of his unique talents, design skills and his personal service. His business has had its ups and downs, its good points and its low points, but his determination and desire to succeed is the secret of its success.

Case study 4: A chiropodist

A chiropodist used the consultancy sessions to increase his client portfolio by attracting younger people to use his services. At the beginning of the sessions he was heavily stuck in the pain cycle because he didn't really know how to help himself. He had already done many, many different jobs and he really felt that chiropody would have provided him with the professionalism that he was looking for from work. Initially it did but his line of work was heavily focused on the older generation whose problems were often too severe to cure. Also although he recognised that he was a lifeline for many of his patients, their need to talk to him was beginning to drain him. Additionally there was the added problem of his income fluctuating when his patients passed away.

The explanation of the pain cycle helped him to pinpoint how he was withdrawing, withholding and becoming depressed by his circumstances. The possibility that he could create what he wanted brought up feelings of intense jealousy about friends or colleagues who did 'have it all' in terms of the car, the house, the job and holidays. He talked about these feelings and worked through them by starting to ask himself what he needed when the feelings cropped up or he felt jealous. He also had to build up a new set of beliefs that would help him to develop his self-confidence.

The section on communication in Step Four helped him to acknowledge that he did want to attract younger patients rather than changing profession and starting off all over again. He focused on creating an image and a profile of a 'foot' specialist who could help, advise and educate people about the care that was needed in order to avoid pitfalls later on. His work became focused on prevention and attention rather than cure.

However, what was interesting about this client is that he did have a number of things to work through. He would go away after each session full of enthusiasm and passion about what he was going to work on and work through. Because he recognised that he had been feeling heavy and lacking enthusiasm, he often used to share the content of the sessions with his mates and family. This often had a knock-on effect, because instead of just buying into this and supporting him they would often ask him tough questions – hence he was put back into the pain cycle. So he found that between sessions he was often on a rollercoaster of emotions, being up one minute and then down the next.

He then had to ask himself exactly what role he was expecting his friends and family to play within his career. The answer was that he wanted them to support and listen to him just as he would listen to his patients. This admission helped him to begin to realise and appreciate his unique talents and that he had to set about supporting himself. Instead of blurting out all the things he was learning about, he began to go quiet and accept that it was often better not to share everything with everyone. This process began to help him to build up his trust in himself. The biggest thing he then noticed was that his job progress increased as he kept quiet and got on with it himself. So slowly but surely this client began to attract younger clients and by working with them he became more fun, light-hearted and forward-thinking himself.

Case study 5: A herbalist

A herbalist used the consultancy sessions to expand her experience of herbal medicine. Her small local store provided only limited exposure to the market. Her burning desire was to be 'more', do 'more' and offer 'more' but what stopped her changing job or direction was her belief that there was always someone who was more experienced and qualified than herself.

The consultancy sessions explored ways in which she could build up her profile by writing articles for magazines and producing an in-house information brochure on ailments and remedies. While she was doing all this, she keep trying to knock herself and argue that she wasn't getting on in her field of work or earning the kind of salary she would have liked. Her issue was time and the fact that she felt she was missing out. She would always tell me about how a friend of hers, who was the same age as her, was doing better than she was. She then needed to explore the beliefs that she had around the 'better than' issue. Was it about money? Was it about glamour? Was it about opportunity? It was about all of these. When she had worked through her issues and created more supportive beliefs she started to investigate the job market.

The key to this was that she was ready to take action and valued herself enough to write a glowing application. A big transition had taken place because at the beginning of the consultancy sessions she had told me how she wanted me to wave a magic wand and to make this dream job appear. When the dream job materialised she was one of a very few who were recognised within the sector who were selected for interview. Everything she had been doing to date was in preparation for her big opportunity and whereas time had been an issue for her it was suddenly irrelevant. She now works for a major organisation promoting their new pilot herbal medicine section. Her desire to reach out and educate more people is providing her with lots of opportunity and, of course, fulfilment.

Case study 6: A teacher

A teacher who felt disappointed, run 'ragged' and frustrated by her pupils' backchat, rudeness and lack of co-operation had arrived at a point in her working life when she no longer felt that she was cut out for teaching. Her job was draining her of her natural enthusiasm and positive approach to life. Her weekends were absorbed with doing schoolwork and her evenings were just about long enough to recover for the next day. The self-development questionnaire helped her to identify how she was allowing her energy to drain and the 30-day programme begrudgingly convinced her that she needed to find 15 minutes for herself each day to do the exercises. The section on 'healing the space' helped her identify that she did want to develop her skills in behavioural management.

She committed to developing this area of her expertise so that she could 'reach out' to the pupils who would previously have left her feeling as if she was banging her head against a brick wall. The course she attended was a practical course that helped her to develop classroom management techniques. The consultancy sessions helped to pinpoint her areas of potential development and allowed her to feel that she still had a lot left to offer her profession and job as well.

Case study 7: An administration worker

An administration worker employed by a local charity used the sessions to accelerate her career and develop her self-confidence. A divorce, illness and the knock-on effects on her self-esteem and confidence had meant that she was doing a job well below her capability. She believed that less stress would help her to cope better and a job that demanded less of her in the day would mean that she would have more energy to do the things she enjoyed at night. Great in theory, but it didn't work out in practice.

Her job, although enjoyable, didn't pay her enough money to

cover all the things she wanted to enjoy in life. This in turn led her to feeling at first that she should just put up with it and then in time to feeling resentful and bitter. She didn't enjoy having to think about what she could afford this month, next month or even next year! She was heavily caught up in the pain cycle when she first came to see me.

The pain cycle, however, had a positive effect on her because it had stimulated her to desire to be earning more money. However, our discussions about money and belief work brought up the issue of whether she deserved more money. She had in effect got used to being 'poor' even though she didn't like it much. So she created lots of new beliefs that she worked on daily, which built up her feelings of self-worth. As she did her daily work, she began to feel comfortable about letting go of past experiences and she began to realise that she wasn't doing herself any favours by keeping her talents hidden. As her confidence grew she began to talk more openly in the office about her skills and capabilities and put herself forward for new projects. As her boss and her colleagues got used to her 'new image' her performance improved. Her efforts were rewarded both by a promotion to a higher-grade job and most importantly by her renewed feelings of self-worth.

Case study 8: An accountant

An accountant used the consultancy sessions to release himself from the rat race and gain more global experience. When he came to the sessions he was full of feelings about, 'Is this really it?' He loved his profession, but his job just wasn't really giving him a buzz, as it had done at the beginning of his career. His work, as he described it, was 'dull and boring'.

His issue was about taking responsibility for his job and career. He was gaining 'Exceeds' in all his appraisals but the directorships and big pay packets didn't seem to be coming his way. Needless to say, he was frustrated and confused about what he needed to do in order to secure a promotion or a pay rise.

The issue about responsibility was a big one because he really liked to be recognised for his valued contribution to the company so he was a bit resistant in the beginning about starting to make things happen for himself. 'Yes, but it won't be the same', he would tell me. 'I won't feel the same way if I have to do all the work myself.' But equally he was unprepared to sit back and wait, and he knew that his frustration was already spilling out in his attitude. He admitted that he was quick to judge or knock his colleagues or associates if he felt irritated. He also admitted that he was a bit of a game-player and would withhold information from certain people in order to get a kick.

Self-reflection for him was about seeing his entire attitude – the good bits and the nasty bits. So he needed to make some changes if he wanted his career to progress. He stopped allowing others within the organisation to lean on him or to draw on his energy, ideas and enthusiasm and he started to hold on to his own energy. He started to work hard on developing himself and creating plans for his future. He started to visualise his contribution to the work world as global and to take the initiative and travel more within his role.

He is achieving his mission to 'make a difference' and is currently living and working in the United States. His sessions helped him to use his own energy constructively and to stop 'lashing out' at others and to keep the focus on his goal or target.

Case study 9: An artist

An artist used the consultancy sessions to rekindle her love of art and texture. She had been lured into doing what she felt was 'the right thing to do', which was to earn a steady income and fit her art in, as and when she could. As you'd expect, her art never got done because there was never time and always lots of other things to do.

During her first session she talked a lot about her amazing confrontation with her past life and how this was arousing all sorts of emotions and uncomfortable feelings within her. These confrontations or 'wake-up calls' were so powerful that whereas before she could just dismiss them, now she no longer felt that she could. She described how she felt that they must have been telling her something, which they were, of course. Her wake-up calls were all connected with art and what was so amazing was that these calls were specific to this client; hence why she found them so unnerving.

- She'd notice lots of new art galleries in her area.
- She'd find herself day-dreaming about her past experiences when she'd done television interviews about her portraits.
- She'd hear herself tell people when they asked her what she did for a living that she was an artist.
- She was asked by an acquaintance to do a portrait painting.
- She'd stumble across pieces of her old work when she was clearing out cupboards.

She told me how these wake-up calls had initially confused her because she thought that her mind was playing tricks on her. She didn't want to go back and do portrait painting as she found it stressful, but it was very important to her that her clients 'loved' her work.

So she described in detail how these wake-up calls made her feel angry. The initial sessions were focused on how she could get a better-paid job, which would then give her more money to spend on materials. My comment, 'But I have heard this before' didn't go down too well. As the sessions progressed we kept coming back to conversations about her 'love of art'.

Her talent had been dormant for 20 years and, yes, it was very painful to admit and acknowledge that she'd created this situation. She described her art in terms of making her feel worthwhile, talented, creative, sensuous and above all original. Her issue was that she didn't know how to combine art with her working life because her artwork would take time to do, promote and then provide her with a steady income. So the whole issue raised feelings of self-doubt and a fear of disappointment. She had been here once before and she didn't want to be hurt again.

However, the focus of the sessions changed and the issue was suddenly 'how' she could do it. Working part-time on both options was the short-term solution, with the option of becoming a full-time artist when the income was sufficient. She therefore secured a local authority grant, which was to be paid back over five years, and reduced her hours with her current employer. Refocusing and redefining her purpose in the field of 'art' created the impetus that was required to balance her two part-time roles.

To become passionate about your job, you need to be a passionate person, so take the plunge and be more loving towards others at work, today. It is worth it.

Index